The Names of God

Books by Andrew Jukes

Four Views of Christ
The Names of God
The Law of the Offerings
Types in Genesis

The
Names
of
God

Discovering God as He Desires to be Known

Andrew Jukes

kregel
PUBLICATIONS

Grand Rapids, MI 49501

The Names of God: Discovering God as He Desires to be Known
by Andrew Jukes

Copyright 1967 by Kregel Publications, a division of Kregel, Inc., P.O. Box 2607, Grand Rapids, MI 49501. Kregel Publications provides trusted, biblical publications for Christian growth and service. Your comments and suggestions are valued.

Library of Congress Catalog Card Number 67-28843

Previously titled: The Names of God in Holy Scripture

ISBN 0-8254-2958-7

Printed in the United States of America

17 / 04 03 02

CONTENTS

" I have manifested thy Name to the men which thou gavest me out of the world; . . . for the words which thou gavest me I have given them. . . . And I have declared unto them thy Name, and will declare it, that the love wherewith thou hast loved me may be in them, and I in them."

St. John xvii. 6, 8, 26.

PREFACE

A WEALTH of priceless material from one of the richest periods of Theological investigation and writing lies hidden from ready access in the pages of books now long out of print. Recent interest in the republication of many of these older works has unlocked the doors to treasure-troves of inestimable worth.

This current century has known little of the skilled pen and dedicated scholarship of Andrew Jukes until just recently. The republication of his *Four Views of Christ* and *The Law Of The Offerings* has enabled a wide audience to become acquainted with his intense spirituality, extensive learning and deeply pious reverence for the Word of God.

The chapters embodied in this work were orginally given as a series of lectures in 1882. The actual material is an expansion of the notes used as the basis for those original addresses. These notes, and the lectures based upon them, however, were the product of a lifetime of study and familiarity with this magnificent theme of the meaning to be found in the names of God.

The book has been reproduced essentially in its original form so that nothing of its own sweep and flow has been lost. The occasionally lengthy and sometimes involved sentences have been retained as demonstrating Jukes' intensity of feeling and characteristic modes of expression.

In a generation characterized by indifference and given to shallowness, the appearance of a work of such depth and scope is a welcome reprieve from the frequent outpourings of the commonplace and trivial which so often bears the stamp of "this is the best I could do in a hurry."

The prayer of the author in the Preface to the original edition shows such depth of devotion and humility of person that it almost demands repeating. "The Lord grant that what is here said may serve to make Him better known. When I have erred on any point, may He forgive it. Where by His grace the truth of His Name and Nature has been opened, to Him be all the praise. Each of His Names strikes but one note of that full chord which shall be heard, when that which is perfect is come, and that which is in part is done away. Meanwhile each separate note, however imperfectly it may be here be heard, may awaken some thought of that harmony in God, which ever is, even if as yet it is above us."

If something of this solemn prayer can be realized through the republication of this excellent old work, then the effort expended on the original production and that consumed in preparing this present form will have been repaid many times over.

— Charles R. Wood

INTRODUCTION

WHAT is the meaning of all the teaching and preaching, which by our Lord's command is continued day by day both in the Church and in the world? It means that there is something which we do not know, which it is very important that we should know, and which we are all slow to learn. What is it that we do not know, which it is so important we should know, and which we are so slow to learn? Only two things: we do not know ourselves: we do not know God. All teaching and preaching are to make us know ourselves and God.

Do we know ourselves? Some of us have gone through colleges and schools, and have learnt this language or studied that science: nay, we may have gone round the world, and seen its peoples, its cities, and great sights, without, like the Prodigal, ever " coming to ourselves." And even when we have " come to ourselves," and so have "come to our Father,"[1] we may still not know our special weakness, and what we might do if tempted, or our strength in Christ, who is our true life, when He is manifested in us. St. Peter, the chief of

[1] St. Luke xv. 17, 20.

the Apostles, is one of the many examples which Holy
Scripture gives us to shew how true disciples, though
they love Christ, and have given up much to follow
Him, may be wholly ignorant of their own weakness,
and of man's true perfecting through death and resurrection.   Who understands the wonderful contradictions which go to make up man ?   At times almost
an angel ; at times a beast or devil : now with aspirations high as heaven ; now with self-love and envy low
as hell.   Who knows himself even as his neighbours
know him ?   Well might the old heathen oracle say,
" Know thyself."   Well might the Psalmist again
and again ask, " Lord what is man ? " [1]

And then as to God, do we know Him ?   Do we
even know our true relation to Him ?   What are our
thoughts about Him ?   Is He for us, or against us ?
Is He friend or foe—a stranger or a Father ?   Can we
trust Him as we trust an earthly friend ?   Or are
those right who call themselves Agnostics, and say,
not only that we do not, but even that we cannot,
really know Him ?   Alas—it is too true : men know
Him not.   But this is not man's proper state.   This
is not the will of God respecting us.

Does the book we call the Bible throw any light
upon our present state of ignorance of God and of
ourselves ?   Does it hold out any remedy for it ?
One of its first lessons is to tell us how man became
what he now is, fallen for a while from God, yet not
forsaken by Him.   Who has not heard the story,

[1] Psalm viii. 4 ; cxliv. 3.

little as it is understood, how a lower creature suggested a falsehood as to God and man,—that God was grudging, in denying that which looked so pleasant to the eyes and good for food,—untrue in saying that if man ate of it he should surely die ;—and as to man, that he should be as God, with his eyes opened, knowing good and evil, if only he would act in self-will and disobedience ? Who has not heard, how, as the result of believing this lie, man learnt that he was naked, and hid himself from God, and sought to cover his nakedness with fig leaves, and his disobedience with excuses ; yet that God sought him with a Call, a Promise, and a Gift,—a Call which is yet sounding in the ears of all, asking man where he now is, and why he is not still with Him who made him,— a Promise also of deliverance from his enemy,—and a Gift to meet his present need.[1] It is all in the Old Book : nay—it is being re-enacted every day ; for the " old man " in us yet repeats old Adam's folly. Men everywhere believe the lie, and hide from God, and seek to cover their shame with pretexts, which still leave them naked after all their labour. And the natural result is, man has hard thoughts of God, and high thoughts of himself. God's character everywhere is gone with man, who has now more faith in creatures than in God, and more pleasure in them than in his Maker. Man's thoughts of Him may be seen in the idols which he has set up to represent Him—some monstrous Moloch or Juggernaut, who

[1] Gen. iii. 1-21.

can look unmoved at the destruction of His creatures.
Even a pantomime therefore, as Augustine says, can
please us more than God.   We would not pass a bag
of money, if we might have it, because we could get
some pleasure from it; but we can pass by God,
morning, noon, and night, for we expect no good or
pleasure from Him.   So we eat without Him, drink
without Him, buy without Him, sell without Him,
live without Him : if we could, we would gladly die
without Him.   For does He not restrict and cross
and punish us all through this fleeting earthly life,
and will He not damn the mass of His poor miserable
creatures at last with endless pain and hell-fire ?
Such is the working of the serpent's lie, which is
rankling deep in every heart, till the remedy, which,
lies as near us as the lie, is by God's Spirit brought
home to us.

For, thank God, there is a remedy, and the remedy
is in God. God is God, spite of His creatures' fall from,
and wretched thoughts of, Him.   All we need is to
know God, and what He truly is, and His relation to
His creatures.   This is the remedy, the only remedy,
for the evil.   Revelation, that is an unveiling of Him,
—for the serpent's lie and its bitter fruits have almost
wholly hidden God from us,—in a word, His shewing
Himself to us as we can bear it,—is the means, not
only to give us peace and bring us to God, but to
change us again into His own image.   Just as the
sun, if it shines upon the earth, changes everything
it shines on,—as the light, if it comes upon the fields,

makes them partakers of its varied hues and bright-
nesses,—so does God's revelation of Himself to His
fallen creature restore in it His likeness. We become like Him just in proportion as we see Him as
He is.

But how has God revealed Himself to man?
Even as man yet reveals himself; for man was made
in God's image. Man shews himself by his words and
works. God in like manner has done this. His Word
is the express image of His person and the brightness of His glory; and by that Word, which is perfect truth, He has answered, and still answers, the
false word of the serpent, which has been our ruin.
By His Word in nature, "for the heavens declare
His glory," [1] though to fallen man there seems "no
voice or language" in them;—by His Word spoken
through His servants, "at sundry times and in divers
manners," [2] coming to us from without and in the
letter, because we could not bear His Spirit;—above
all by His "Word made flesh," in Christ our Lord; [3]
—God has shewn us what He is, and thus by word
and deed answered the lie that He is grudging and
untrue, and that man can be as God in independence of Him. Does not God love? Is He not
true? Christ is the answer. God is so loving, that,
though His creature has fallen, He will come into
his likeness for him, and will lift up man again to
bear His own image. God is so true, that, if man
sins, he must surely die. But God through death

---

[1] Psalm xix. 1.   [2] Heb. i. 1.   [3] St. John i. 14.

can destroy him that has the power of death, and
say to death, "I will be thy plagues, and to hell, I
will be thy destruction." [1]   Nay, He has already done
it for us in Jesus Christ our Lord.   Christ shews us
man condemned, and yet justified.   God has dwelt
in man, born of a woman, in all the fulness of the
Godhead bodily; [2] and man, who has suffered and
died, now dwells in God, with all power in heaven and
earth, to destroy the works of the devil, and to reconcile and bring back all to God for ever. [3]   This is
God's answer to the serpent's lie.   The Word has
been made flesh. [4]   God has taken on Him the curse,
that man should be blessed, and bear His image
evermore.

The perfect revelation then of God is in Jesus
Christ our Lord.   But the very fulness of the revelation, like the dazzling brightness of the sun, may
keep us for a while from seeing all its wonders; and
we may learn, even from the revelation in the letter,
that is from Holy Scripture, specially from the varied
names under which it has pleased God to reveal Himself to man from the beginning, things concerning
His nature and fulness, which, though they are all
more perfectly revealed in Christ, would perhaps be
beyond our vision but for the help which even the
shadows of the letter give us.   What have men not
learnt from the shadow of the earth upon the moon.
So the old revelation which God has given us of Him-

---

[1] Hos. xiii. 14.

[2] Col. ii. 9.

[3] Col. i. 20.

[4] St. John i. 14.

self in Holy Scripture, as "God," or "LORD," or "Almighty," or the "Most High," though it is "piece-meal," [1] as the Apostle says, may assist us, to see His fulness; just as the many figures which the same Scriptures give us, in the carnal offerings of the ceremonial law, help us to see the varied and apparently contradictory aspects of the one great perfect Sacrifice. We cannot yet see the things of heaven. God therefore reveals them as we can bear it, with the accuracy of One who sees them as they are, and in a way in which they may be seen and understood by us. And we need all His teaching, even the partial revelations, which represent Him under varied names, by which He prepares us in due time to see Him as He is,[2] and to know as we are known.[3]

I purpose therefore, if God permit, to call attention to the names under which God has revealed Himself to man in Holy Scripture. The first four we find in the earlier chapters of Genesis. They are, first, "God," (in Hebrew, Elohim;) then, "LORD," (or Jehovah;) then, "Almighty," (El Shaddai;) and then, "Most High," (El Elyon.) These all reveal some distinct attribute or characteristic of the same one blessed God. Beside these we have three other names, which describe God's relation to certain things or persons rather than His nature; namely "Lord," (in Hebrew Adonai;) then "The Everlasting God," (El Olam;) and lastly,

---

[1] Heb. i. 1.   [2] 1 St. John iii. 2.

[3] 1 Cor. xiii. 12.

" Lord of Hosts," (Jehovah Sabaoth.) But the first
four names tell us what God is. In every age these
first four names have been the rest and refuge and
comfort of His people. In the book of Psalms we
find them all constantly repeated : in one place we
have all four within the compass of a single sentence :—" He that dwelleth in the secret place of the
MOST HIGH, shall abide under the shadow of the
ALMIGHTY. I will say of the LORD, (that is Jehovah,)
He is my refuge and my fortress; my GOD, (that is
my Elohim,) in Him will I trust." [1] All these varying
names are but the result of His being what He is,
so wonderful and manifold, that no one name can
adequately express what an apostle calls His " fulness." [2] Just as in the Gospels four distinct and
varying presentations of the same One Lord, as the
Lion, the Ox, the Man, the Eagle, are required to
shew the Christ in all His varied aspects or relations,
some of which, as we here apprehend them, under
the limitations of our fallen nature, seem at times to
clash with other no less true views of Him who is
both Son of God and Son of Man; while it is no
less true that in each distinct presentation of Him
we may detect hidden intimations that He contains
within Himself all the apparently varying characteristics, which the other Gospels or Cherubic Faces
reveal more particularly ; [3] so is it in the older revela-

---

[1] Psalm xci. 1, 2; so too in Psalm lxxvii. 7–11, we have four
names.   [2] Eph. iii. 19; Col. i. 19; ii. 9.

[3] See *Four Views of Christ*, pp. 2-14.

tion, which God gave of Himself. He cannot fully speak of Himself under a single name or under one title. And yet each differing name contains, hidden in itself, (for God's perfections are inseparable,) something of the special virtues which the other names bring out more separately. We may see this even in a man of varied gifts. To know David we must be told that he was Shepherd, Warrior, King, Prophet, Poet, and Musician. All these are outcomes of a deep and rich nature. Shall we then wonder that God, the Maker, Judge, and Saviour of all, who in Himself is Love, and Power, and Wisdom, if He is to reveal His nature and relationships to those who know Him not, must be known by many names, each of which can only tell out something of His glory. At all events, God has thus revealed Himself to man, here a little, and there a little; and His children, as they grow up into His likeness, can only bless and praise Him for such a revelation.

My desire, then, in considering the names under which God has revealed Himself, is by them to lead some of His children and His creatures, if it may be so, to learn to know Him better. But indirectly and incidentally our study of this subject may also answer the objections of certain critics, who, from the varied names of God in Genesis, have argued that the book is a merely human composition, based on and compiled from several earlier and conflicting records, the differences and divergences of which shew that they are only the views or speculations of fallible minds as to the nature and character of God. If these critics, whose criticisms I may say are continually destroying one another, instead of so confidently judging that " Scripture," which our Lord says " cannot be broken,"[1] could have only more deeply considered the question how God can reveal Himself to fallen creatures, and whether it is possible, while they are as they are, to make them know Him fully as He is,—still more if they could have been " disciples," that is learners in the school, of Christ, before they set up to be teachers,—they might, and I believe would, have learnt the reason for the form of the revelation which God has given us in Holy Scripture. Surely from the beginning, seeing what man had become, God must have desired to make Himself known ; and being All-loving and All-wise, He cannot but have taken the best method of doing it. But how could He do it, man being what he is ? What can we shew of our nature to an infant child ? What can we make a beast understand of our inward thoughts and feelings ? Was it not a simple necessity of the case that God should shew Himself under many forms, and according to the limitations of the creature in and to whom He sought to reveal Himself ? Was it not necessary that the revelation should be in creature form and grow from stage to stage, even as Christ, the Word

---

[1] St. John x. 25.

of God, when He was made flesh for us, grew in wisdom and stature unto the perfect man ?[1]

The fact therefore, supposing it to be a fact, that those portions of the book of Genesis which speak of " Elohim " were part of an earlier or a later record than those which tell us of " Jehovah," can never prove that in its present form and order this book and the rest of Holy Scripture are not divinely given to us. In an elaborate mosaic the bits of stone have come from different quarries, but the pattern or figure which is formed by them shews that the work is not a mere chance collection of discordant atoms, but that a superintending mind has arranged and planned it with a special purpose. The fact too, which chemistry has proved, that the substances of which our flesh and bones are formed were all in the earth, and then in animal or vegetable forms, before they became parts of our present earthly bodies, is no disproof that these bodies are the work of God, or their form and arrangement the result of His purpose. So with the Bible. Even if it could be shewn that some portions of it have come from a record treasured by those who knew God only as " Elohim," while some other part was originally the vision granted to those who knew Him rather as " Jehovah," (which is not impossible, though it has not yet been proved,) such a fact, if it be a fact, would militate nothing against the unity or Divine inspiration of Holy Scripture as we now

[1] St. Luke ii. 52.

have it, but would only shew, what Scripture itself
asserts, that God has spoken to man through partial
revelations, till he could receive a more perfect knowledge of the truth through Christ and His Spirit.

Of course in such a case, if men are not aware
of their state as fallen from God, and as such unable
to see Him as He is, it is easy to object that one
partial presentation or revelation of Him contradicts
or clashes with another. But all nature is full of
similar apparent contradictions, which are found to
be no contradictions, as its secrets one by one are
opened to us. Is not the one white light made up of
seven differing rays and colours ? Is not the order of
the heavens, so quiet and so firm, the result of forces,
centrifugal and centripetal, which seem directly antagonistic ? Is not the balance of the heart's life preserved by systole and diastole ? Is not the unity
of mankind made up of man and woman ? In the
moral world it is the same. Truth seems often opposed to love ; yet are truth and love both outcomes
and manifestations of the same one Blessed God.
Christ, the perfect image of God, reveals to us the
unity of all apparent antagonisms. While however
we remain in the flesh, we can only " know in
part," [1] and to meet us with such knowledge, He,
whose fulness fills all things, has revealed Himself
in a way which men may call imperfect, the very
imperfection of which, if it may be called so, is
its perfection, shewing its perfect adaptation for its

[1] 1 Cor. xiii. 12.

appointed end. If we can but see what the differing names of God declare, we shall be forced, I feel assured, like all who have seen this great sight, to fall down before Him, crying, " Holy, Holy, Holy, Lord, God, Almighty, Most High, heaven and earth are full of the majesty of thy glory."

I will only add here, that, as these names of God speak of His nature, none can ever rightly see their import but those who are partakers of that nature ; " for who knoweth the things of a man, save the spirit of man which is in him ? even so the things of God knoweth no man, but the Spirit of God." Mere intellect therefore will never open what these names contain, nor will even the desire for light, unless that desire is joined with faith and prayer and humility. On the other hand a walk of faith, a life of love, a daily waiting upon God for His Spirit, a humble treasuring of His words, even when at first they seem dark and mysterious, these things, as they come from God, will lead to God, and to a fuller knowledge of Him, and of His fulness, as He has revealed it in His written and in His Incarnate Word. He has made us to know and love Him, and to bear His image, and so to reveal Him to a world which knows Him not. And just as by grace that image is restored in us, by the indwelling of Him who is the image of the invisible God, we may see what eye hath not seen, and hear what ear hath not heard, even the things which God reveals by His Spirit. There is indeed a stage of our experience, when the one question

which occupies the soul is, How can a sinner be
brought to righteousness and peace? But there is
no less surely another, in which the soul hungers
after God, to know Him and His perfections, in the
deep sense that to know Him is the way to be conformed to Him. The names of God serve both these
ends. In the beatific vision God will be all. Even
here, in proportion as His redeemed see Him, they
are made like Him. May our meditations on His
names serve this end, to His glory and our blessing
evermore!

1

GOD OR ELOHIM

HAVING thus seen that in Holy Scripture God is spoken of under different names, each given with a purpose, to set forth some distinct virtue or characteristic of His nature, we may now turn to the first name under which He is revealed. This is " God," —in Hebrew, " Elohim." [1] This is the name, and the only name, by which God is set before us in the first chapter of the book of Genesis. Here we find it repeated in almost every verse. Under this name we see God, according to His own will, working on a dark and ruined creature, till by His Word all is set in order and made "very good." This is the name which we need to know before all others. This, therefore, is the first revealed in Holy Scripture ; for it shews us One, who, when all is lost, in darkness and confusion, brings back, first His light and life, and then His image, into the creature, and so makes all things new and very good.

Now there are certain peculiarities connected with this name, which must be considered, if we would understand even in measure all that is divinely taught under it.

[1] Heb. אלהים.

This name then, (in Hebrew, " Elohim " or
" Alehim,") is a plural noun, which, though first and
primarily used in Holy Scripture to describe the One
true God, our Creator and Redeemer, is used also in a
lower sense in reference to the " gods many and lords
many," [1] whom the ancient heathen feared and worshipped.　Let us first look at the primary use of
this name, in which we learn its highest significance.
We shall then better understand how it could be
applied to the gods of the heathen, or to the idols
which represented them.

First then this name, though a plural noun, when
used of the one true God is constantly joined with
verbs and adjectives in the singular.[2]　We are thus
prepared, even from the beginning, for the mystery
of a plurality in God, who, though He says, " There
is no God beside me," [3] and " I am God, and there is
none else," [4] says also, " Let us make man in our
image, after our likeness ; " [5] and again, " The man is
become like one of us ; " [6] and again at Babel, " Go
to, let us go down and confound their language ; " [7]
and again, in the vision granted to the prophet
Isaiah, " Whom shall I send, and who will go for
us." [8]　And this same mystery, though hidden from
an English reader, comes out again and again in

---

[1] 1 Cor. viii. 5.

[2] For singular *verbs* with Elohim, see Gen. i. 1, 3, &c., and in
countless places.　For singular *adjectives* see 2 Kings xix. 4, 16 ;
Psalm vii. 9, Psalm lvii. 2, &c. (see Gesenius, *Thesaurus*, under
אלהים, p. 96.)

[3] Deut. xxxii. 39.　　[4] Isa. xlv. 5, 22.　　[5] Gen. i. 26.
[6] Gen. iii. 22.　　[7] Gen. xi. 7.　　[8] Isa. vi. 6,

many other texts of Holy Scripture. For " Remember thy Creator in the days of thy youth," is literally, " Remember thy Creators." [1] Again, " None saith, Where is God my Maker ? " is in the Hebrew, " God my Makers." [2] So again, " Let Israel rejoice in Him that made him," is, in the Hebrew, " in his Makers." [3] And so again in the Proverbs, " The knowledge of the Holy Ones is understanding." [4] So again where the Prophet says, " Thy Maker is thy husband," both words are plural in the Hebrew.[5] Many other passages of Scripture have precisely the same peculiarity.[6] Therefore in heaven " Cherubim and Seraphim continually do cry, Holy, Holy, Holy, LORD of Hosts," [7] while on earth, taught by the Spirit of our Lord, we say, " Father, Son, and Holy Ghost." [8] The plural form of the first name of God, that is " Elohim," shadows forth the same mystery ; while the verb, and even the adjective, joined with it in the singular, as when we read, " the living," [9] or " the righteous," [10] or " the Most High God," [11] shew that this " Elohim," though plural, is but One God.[12]

---

[1] Eccl. xii. 1. [2] Job xxxv. 10.

[3] Psalm cxlix. 2. [4] Prov. ix. 10. [5] Isa. liv. 5.

[6] For example, " Holy Ones " in Job v. 1, and in Hos. xi. 12 ; and " Thy Redeemers " in Isa. xliv. 24, &c.

[7] Isa. vi. 3 ; Rev. iv. 8. [8] 2 Cor. xiii. 14.

[9] 2 Kings xix. 4, 10 ; Heb. אלהים הי.

[10] Psalm vii. 9 ; Heb. אלהים צדיק.

[11] Psalm lvii. 2 ; Heb. אלהים עליון. See Gesenius, *Thesaurus*, p. 96, under אלהים.

[12] In a very few places this name, " Elohim," is joined with

Further, this name, like every other name in the
Hebrew, has a distinct meaning, full of significance.
For the word " Elohim " [1] is formed from the Hebrew
word, " Alah," [2] " to swear," and describes One who
stands in a covenant-relationship, which is ratified
by an oath. Parkhurst, in his well-known Lexicon,
thus explains the name :—" Elohim : " " A name
usually given in the Hebrew Scriptures to the ever-
blessed Trinity, by which they represent themselves
as under the obligation of an oath. . . . This oath,
(referred to in Psalm cx. 4, ' The Lord sware and
will not repent,') was prior to creation. Accordingly ' Jehovah ' is at the beginning of the creation
called ' Elohim,' in Gen. i. 1, which implies that the
Divine Persons had sworn when they created ; and it
is evident, from Gen. iii. 4, 5, that both the Serpent
and the Woman knew ' Jehovah ' by this name,
' Elohim,' before the Fall." [3] Here a wondrous deep

---

plural adjectives, (see Gen. xx. 13 ; xxxv. 7 ;) and verbs, (Deut. iv.
7 ; v. 26 ; Josh xxiv. 19 ; 1 Sam. xvii. 26, 36 ; 2 Sam. vii. 23 ; Psalm
lviii. 12 ; Jer. x. 10 ; xxiii. 36.) But in all these cases, except
the first two, where perhaps angels are referred to, the name
" Jehovah " is connected with " Elohim ; " and the plural adjective
or verb may be used to teach us, that in the One " Jehovah "
there is the plurality of the " Elohim."

[1] Heb. אלהים.   [2] Heb. אלה.

[3] Parkhurst adds here, " From this name (Elohim) of the true
God, the Greeks had their Ζεὺς ὅρκιος. Hence, also, the corrupt
tradition of Jupiter's oath, which overruled even Fate itself "
(*Heb. Lex.* in loc.). As to the view of some, that the word
" Elohim " is derived directly from El, (אל) which signifies
" strong" or "mighty," it may perhaps suffice to say that the plural
of El is Elim, not Elohim. God surely may be and is called both

opens to our view, as to the nature and being of God. Blessed be His name, that He has Himself, both by His Son and by His Spirit, given us some glimpses into the height and the depth here set before us, which flesh and blood never could have fathomed.

For this covenant-relationship, which the name " Elohim " expresses, is first a relationship in God. He is One, but in Him also, as His name declares, there is plurality; and in this plurality He has certain relationships, both in and with Himself, which, because He is God, can never be dissolved or broken. Thus, as Parkhurst says, this name contains the mystery of the Trinity. For the perfect revelation of this great mystery man had indeed to wait until it was declared by the Only-begotten of the Father, and even then only after His resurrection from the dead, to those whom He had called to be His disciples. But from the beginning the name " Elohim " contained and shadowed it forth, and the visions and words of the prophets gave still clearer intimations of it.

Into this mystery, however, I do not here enter,

" El," (Gen. xiv. 20, and in many other places,) and " Elim," (as in Psalm xxix. 1; and elsewhere,) that is " The Mighty;" but the letter H in " Elohim " points to the true etymology of the name, as from אלה, " to swear "; though, indeed, אלה is also probably connected with אל; for, as the Apostle says, (Heb. vi. 16,) " Men verily swear by the greater;" and the original idea of an oath may have been this affirmation by the " Strong " or " Mighty One." In the case of God, as the same Apostle writes, " Because He could swear by no greater, He sware by Himself." (Heb. vi. 13.)

further than to say, with St. Augustine, that, if God is love, then in God there must be a Lover, a Beloved, and the Spirit of love, for there can be no love without a lover and a beloved.[1] And if God be eternal, then there must be an eternal Lover, and an eternal Beloved, and an eternal Spirit of Love, which unites the eternal Lover to the eternal Beloved, in a bond of Love which is eternal and indissoluble. The relationship in God, in and with Himself, is one in which there can be no breach. From the beginning God is " Elohim," in covenant-union with Himself for evermore.

But the truth here, as to the covenant-relationship involved in the name " Elohim," goes still further. For the Beloved is the Son, "the Word," " by whom all things were made," and " in whom all things consist." " All things were created by Him and for Him." [2] God therefore, or " Elohim," in covenant with the Beloved Son, must be in covenant with all that is created by Him, and which only consists, or is held together, in Him. For, as St. Paul says, He is " the God who cannot lie, who promised eternal life before the world began," [3]—words which again refer to the covenant in Christ before the Fall :—" the Faithful Creator," as St. Peter adds, to whom we may " commit the keeping of our souls ; " [4] for " Of Him, and through Him, and to Him are all things." [5] And in virtue of this covenant-relationship, because He

---

[1] " Ubi amor, ibi trinitas." See Augustine, *De Trinitate*, lib. viii. cap. 10; lib. ix. cap. 2 ; and lib. xv. cap. 3.

[2] St. John i. 3 ; and Col. i. 16, 17.   [3] Titus i. 2.

[4] 1 Pet. iv. 19.   [5] Rom. xi. 36.

is " Elohim," though His creatures fail and fall, " He will never leave us, nor forsake us."

It may be asked, whether, when this name was first revealed, those who received it could have understood all that was thus implicitly contained in and taught by it. Probably they did not. When God first speaks, men rarely, if ever, fully understand Him. It is only by degrees, and just in proportion as His servants and disciples treasure up His words and seek to obey Him, that those words, often very slowly, open to them. All our first apprehensions of Him and of His truth are imperfect, and mixed with fallacies arising from the senses. Nevertheless His words, even when little understood, convey true blessing to those who receive them, though the depths of Divine wisdom which they contain are more or less hidden. Who at first takes in all that Nature is saying to us ? Who, when he first receives the Gospel or the Sacraments of the Gospel, understands all that they convey and witness to him ? And so with the names of God. Though even yet little understood, from the beginning they have been telling what God's fulness is, and through His grace telling it in such ways and in such measures as fallen men were able to receive and profit by. Just in proportion as they walked with Him, His names and words would open to them, while, if they forsook Him, the selfsame words would first be dark and then perverted to misrepresent Him. For the Word of God, if not obeyed, ever becomes a curse and snare, even confirming men in their worst errors and delusions.

It was so with this first and wondrous name, "Elohim." The truth it taught was soon abused and turned into a lie, as man departed more and more from God, and in His place "worshipped and served the creature more than the Creator." For the truth, that in "Elohim," who says, "There is no God beside me," there is plurality, was soon perverted into many gods; the manifold and diverse powers in nature, which had been formed to shew forth God's fulness, being worshipped as so many distinct and differing deities; and then His covenant-relation to His creatures was made the ground of the doctrine, that each nation or people had its tutelary gods, who stood in special relationship to those who acknowledged and served them. Thus each country had its own gods, some the "gods of the hills," some those "of the valleys," [1] each of which was worshipped as more or less intimately related to different lands or peoples. For, looking at nature, fallen man saw power or force on every hand : power in the sun, which seemed to make the earth bring forth and bud : power in the earth to support and nourish all creatures : power in the sea, and in the air; in cold and lightning, and storm. Each of these seemed stronger than man : some served him at times, but could also cross and wound and slay him. So man, having let go the faith that God is Love, bowed to the powers which were around him, and looked to them and worshipped them as gods. Is there no

---

[1] Judges x. 6 ; 1 Kings xi. 33 ; and xx. 23, 28.

such worship even now? Alas, the world always does this. For a worshipper by his very constitution man must be. And if he cannot trust a God of Love and Truth, the true "Elohim," he will surely look for help to some of the forces, seen or unseen, which compass him on every hand.[1]

But to return to the name, "Elohim," as used in Holy Scripture of the One true God. The whole first chapter of Genesis shews us One, who, because He is "Elohim," in virtue of His own nature and covenant-relation to His creature, can never leave it, fallen as it is, till all again is very good. In that opening chapter, which is indeed the foundation and sum of all further revelation, we are told of a creation, by "Elohim," of the heavens and the earth ; and then that creation, or part of it at least, is shewn as fallen, "without form and void," with "darkness upon the face of the deep." But does "Elohim" forsake it because it has become dark and void and formless? No. When nothing else moves, "the Spirit of God moves," (literally, "broods,") "over the face of the waters," and then "Elohim" speaks, and by His Word, step by step, the wondrous change

---

[1] Parkhurst, in his note on the secondary sense of the word, "Elohim," as applied to the gods or powers which the heathen worshipped, says, "The ancient heathen called, not only the whole heaven, but any one of its three conditions, (namely fire, light, and air or spirit,) 'Elohim.' They meant not to deny the joint action of the material trinity, but to give it the glory of each particular attribute. See Hutchinson's *Trinity of the Gentiles*, p. 246 ; and also his *Moses sine Principio*, p. 116."

is wrought, till the day of rest is reached, when " all is very good."

For the fallen creature begins nothing, continues nothing, perfects nothing. Each stage of the restoration is the direct result of the unsought word and work of " Elohim." At every step again and again we read, " God said," and " God made." [1] Throughout, all is of God, whose name and nature in itself contains the pledge that He cannot rest till His fallen creature is restored and re-created. No wonder then that the early Church dwelt so much and often on the work of the Six Days,[2] seeing in them a covenant-God, whose new creation from first to last is wholly His workmanship. And what a work it is ! First " Elohim" by His word brings " light." Then a "heaven" is formed in the yet restless creature, to divide the waters from the waters. Then a rising " earth " is seen emerging from the waters. Then come " fruits ; " then "lights;" then "living creatures," first from the waters, then from the earth; till at last the "man" is created in the image of God to have dominion over all. Nothing hinders His work or changes His purpose. Again and again, even after He begins His work, the awful darkness rises for awhile, and in each returning " evening " seems to swallow up the light; but again and again the covenant-God, " Elohim," binds the darkness every " morning," and even incorporates it into " days " of ever-progressing blessing, for it is

---

[1] Gen. i. 3, 6, 7, 9, 11, 16, &c.

[2] Almost all the Great Fathers have left us their *Hexemerons*.

written, " The evening and the morning made the
day," until the seventh day comes, when we read of
no " evening." Blessed be God, not a few by grace
know all these stages in their own experience. They
know, that, until the Word has spoken, there is no
light in them by which to see their ruin. What
barren restless waters does the light at first reveal.
But the very discovery of the barrenness is progress.
Till this is seen, no heaven is formed. Till the heaven
is formed, the earth can yield no fruits or increase.
Till the fruits appear, there are no lights in heaven,
to rule the day and to rule the night, nor living
creatures either from the waters or the earth. Every
stage is a preparation for something yet more perfect.
It is only as we know our need that we really know
God. And by His work in us He makes us know
what it is to have a covenant-God, whose fulness
meets our every want, and whose very name and
nature is the pledge of our deliverance.

And mark especially that " Elohim " works, not
only *on*, but *with*, the creature. This indeed is
grace, most wondrous and abounding. For it is all
of grace that " Elohim " should restore and save His
fallen creature. It is still greater grace that in the
restoration He makes that creature a fellow-worker
with Himself. Yet so it is. For He says, " Let the
waters bring forth," and " Let the earth bring forth." [1]
In other words He calls the fallen creature to travail
and labour with Him. His love indeed is the cause

[1] Gen. i. 11, 20, 24.

of all, and His Word the agent in effecting all; but in accomplishing His purpose He works, not apart from, but with, the creature. Herein is the root of the truth which lies in the doctrine of Evolution. For it is not that Nature, unaided or apart from God, can re-create or change herself, or by herself evolve ever-advancing forms of life, all leading up to man in God's image; but rather, that, even in her lowest fall, God accepts the captive powers of the fallen creature, as a matrix from which, through successive births, all quickened by His Word, He may, according to her advancing state, bring forth advancing forms of life, each shewing some nearer resemblance to His image. And the fact that this earth, when God began to work upon it, was itself the ruin of a prior creation,[1]—the debris, if I mistake not, of the once bright spiritual kingdom of Satan and his angels, destroyed and self-consumed by him,—may explain what seems so perplexing, namely that there should be in all nature, what some have called " a concausation of evil." [2]   God certainly adopted

---

[1] In Isaiah xlv. 18, God distinctly says that He did not create the earth "without form;" in Hebrew, "tohu," תֹהוּ. The formlessness was the result of some fall.

[2] John Stuart Mill constantly repeats this thought, that in nature, not only do we see the presence both of good and evil, but further, that the evil is *working with the good*, in the composition of things as they now are; which to him appears a proof that nature cannot be the work of a perfectly good and powerful God. See his *Essay on Nature*, almost *passim*; and the second part of the *Essay on Theism*, entitled *Attributes*, pp. 184, 185, 186.

the darkness of each returning "evening," and in-
corporated it into "days" of ever growing order,
until the seventh day comes without an evening.
Had not the "earth" and "waters" also germs in
them of their fallen and corrupted nature, and do
not these manifest themselves, even when they are
commanded by Elohim to bring forth new life?
Certainly in our regeneration we see how the old
man shews himself, and is even stimulated by the
Word, which brings new and strange forms of life
out of the fallen creature. Such a working shews
what "Elohim" is, who in His faithfulness and
grace bears with imperfect forms of life, the dumb
"fish" and "creeping thing," until He Himself
"creates"[1] the man in His own image, when "all
is very good." It has ever been so: Moses before
Christ; the flesh or letter before the Spirit; yet both
of God, and shewing forth His grace, who works not
only on, but with, the creature.

Such is the light which the opening chapter of
the book of Genesis throws on the special meaning
of the first name of God, "Elohim." Fully to illus-
trate its import would require an examination of
every passage, where this name occurs in Holy
Scripture. But to attempt this here would be impossible.[2] Nor is it necessary. Any careful reader,
once in possession of the key which the Hebrew

---

[1] Gen. i. 27.

[2] The name "Elohim" occurs about two thousand two hundred and fifty times in the Old Testament.

name carries in itself, can test how the idea conveyed by it is always that of "One in covenant." A selection of texts would only give a part of the evidence. But I may cite a few to shew how distinctly this name, "Elohim," refers to and implies One who stands in a covenant-relationship.

Take the following as examples. First, God's words to Noah:—"And Elohim said unto Noah, The end of all flesh is come before me, . . . but with thee will I establish my covenant."[1] "And I, behold I, establish my covenant with you, and with your seed, and with every living creature that is with you. And this is the token of the covenant which I make between me and you. I do set my bow in the cloud, and I will remember my covenant, which is between me and you and every living creature of all flesh that is upon the earth."[2] So in His words to Abram, "Elohim's" name pledges the same relationship:—"I am the Almighty God: walk before me and be thou perfect; and I will establish my covenant between me and thee, and thy seed after thee in all generations, to be a God to thee, and to thy seed, and I will be their Elohim," that is, I will be with them in covenant-relationship.[3] Therefore again and again we read that "Elohim remembered:"—"Elohim remembered Noah;"[4] and again, "When God destroyed the cities of the plain, Elohim remembered Abram, and sent Lot out of the midst

---

[1] Gen. vi. 13, 18.

[2] Gen. ix. 9, 17.

[3] Gen. xvii. 1–8.

[4] Gen. viii. 1.

of the overthrow;"¹ and again, "Elohim remembered Rachel."² There is the same reference to a covenant in God's words to Isaac,³ and to Jacob;⁴ and Joseph's dying words witness to the same :—"I die, but Elohim will surely visit you, and bring you out of this land, into the land which He sware to Abraham, to Isaac, and to Jacob."⁵ Moses no less refers to it.⁶ David's joy too in the LORD, his God, is, that "He will ever be mindful of His covenant."⁷ Therefore in His deepest trials he "encourages himself in God," saying, "O my soul, hope thou in God, who is the health of my countenance and my God."⁸ His "last words" dwell on the same theme : "Although my house be not so with God, yet hath He made with me an everlasting covenant, ordered in all things and sure ;"⁹ for "Jehovah Elohim" had said, "My mercy will I keep for him for ever, and my covenant shall stand fast with him."¹⁰ It is the same with all the saints. The fact that God is "Elohim," that is the "One who keepeth covenant,"¹¹ is the foundation of His creature's hope in every extremity. "God is our refuge and strength."¹² "He is my God, and my father's God."¹³ And "He hath said, I will never leave thee, nor forsake thee."¹⁴

---

¹ Gen. xix. 29.   ² Gen. xxx. 22 ; also Exod. ii. 24.

³ Gen. xxvi. 24.   ⁴ Gen. xxviii. 13, 14.

⁵ Gen. l. 24.   ⁶ Exod. vi. 2, 3, 4, 7, 8; and Deut. vii. 9.

⁷ Psalm cxi. 5.   ⁸ Psalm xlii. 5, 11.

⁹ 2 Sam. xxiii. 1, 3, 5.   ¹⁰ Psalm lxxxix. 8, 28.

¹¹ 1 Kings viii. 23.   ¹² Psalm xlvi. 1.

¹³ Exod. xv. 2.   ¹⁴ Gen. xxviii. 13, 15 ; and Heb. xiii. 5.

For " He is God of gods, and Lord of lords: He doth execute the judgment of the fatherless and the widow." [1] " A father of the fatherless, and a judge of the widows, is God, in His holy habitation." [2] The faithful Creator [3] cannot fail His creatures. They may be, and are, unworthy, but He is " Elohim " for evermore. Therefore He says, " Look unto me, and be ye saved, all the ends of the earth; for there is no Elohim besides me. I have sworn by myself, the word has gone out of my mouth in righteousness, and shall not return, that unto me every knee shall bow and every tongue shall swear." [4]

And this is the truth, which, above all others, the Gospel opens, in the life and ways of Him who is " the image of the invisible God," [5] who has come to reveal to us a Father's love, which cannot fail because we are " His offspring." [6] We may need another view of God, as the One who " loves righteousness and hates iniquity," and who therefore must judge all evil,[7] till it is destroyed, and " mortality is swallowed up of life." [8] And this, as we shall see, is the special lesson of the second name of God, "Jehovah." But, before and beneath and beyond all this, God yet is " Elohim," that is, God, in covenant. His creatures may not know it. Even His Church may very dimly see it. But God has said, " My covenant

---

[1] Deut. x. 17.
[2] Psalm lxviii. 5.
[3] 1 Pet. iv. 19.
[4] Isa. xlv. 22, 23.
[5] Col. i. 15; Heb. i. 3.
[6] Acts xvii. 28.
[7] Heb. x. 30.
[8] 2 Cor. v. 4.

will I not break, nor alter the word that is gone out of my lips." [1]   Well may Paul argue, " Though it be but a man's covenant, yet, if it be confirmed, no man disannulleth or addeth thereto." Seen as " Jehovah," God may give law; and " the law worketh wrath; for where there is no law, there is no transgression." [2]   But " the covenant which was confirmed before of God in, or to,[3] Christ, the law which was four hundred years after cannot disannul, that it should make the promise of none effect." [4]   The law was needed in its place, to shew the creature what it is, and to slay in man the fallen life of independence. But " the ministration of death and condemnation " is " to be done away," while " the ministration of righteousness and life remaineth." [5]   So the Apostle says again, even of those who slew and rejected Christ, " God is able to graff them in again. . . . For this is my covenant with them, when I shall take away their sins. As concerning the Gospel, they are enemies for your sakes; but as touching the election, they are beloved for the fathers' sakes. For the gifts and calling of God are without repentance. . . . And God hath concluded all in unbelief, that He might have mercy upon all. O the depth of the riches, both of the wisdom and knowledge of God; . . . for of Him, and through Him, and to Him, are all things." [6]

This is what the name " God," or " Elohim,"

---

[1] Psalm lxxxix. 34.   [2] Rom. iv. 15.   [3] Gr. εἰς Χριστόν.
[4] Gal. iii. 15–18.   [5] 2 Cor. iii. 7–11.   [6] Rom. xi. 23–36.

brings out so fully, in itself forestalling not a little of that which we now call the Gospel: this is what the ever-blessed God would teach us, when He assures us that He will be "our God." [1] "For this is the covenant, . . . I will put my laws into their minds, and in their heart will I write them; and I will be unto them a God, and they shall be to me a people." [2] In a word, God promises for both, saying not only, "I will," but "They shall," that is, pledging His word both for Himself and for His creatures. Our Lord's own teaching only repeats the selfsame truth, in those blessed words, even yet so little understood, to Pharisees and Scribes, who objected that He "received sinners." [3] "What man of you," He says, fallen and wretched as you are, would be content to lose even a sheep, which had strayed and wandered from him? Or what woman would be content to lose a piece of silver? Would they not seek their lost until they found it? Is God's love for His creature less than a man's is for a sheep? Is not the lost creature really God's loss? Can He rest, when it is lost, until He find it? And when it is found, is it not His joy even more than the recovered creature's? For it is not the joy of the recovered sheep, nor of the silver, nor of the once lost son, that our Lord declares in these Parables, but the joy of the Shepherd, and of the Woman, and of the Father, each of whom

---

[1] Isa. xl. 1; Jer. vii. 23; xi. 4; xxx. 22; Ezek. xxxiv. 31; and xxxv. 28, &c.

[2] Heb. viii. 10.   [3] St. Luke xv. 1, 2, &c.

exclaims, " Rejoice with me, for I have found that which I had lost." The name " Elohim " says all this, and more also. It says that " God has sworn." [1] It declares that " God, willing more abundantly to shew to the heirs of promise the immutability of His counsel, confirmed it by an oath, that by two immutable things, (His will and His word,) in which it was impossible for God to lie, we might have strong consolation who have fled for refuge to lay hold upon the hope set before us." [2] This is our refuge :—" God is not a man, that He should lie, or the son of man, that He should repent. Hath He said, and shall He not do it ? or hath He spoken, and shall He not make it good ? " [3] Herein is the creature's hope. God is and shall be God for ever. A " great voice from heaven " has said, " Behold, the tabernacle of God is with men, and God Himself shall be with them, and be their God ; and God shall wipe away all tears from their eyes, and there shall be no more death, nor sorrow, nor crying, neither shall there be any more pain, for the former things are passed away." [4]

Such is the first name of God which Holy Scripture gives us. What has here been said in illustration of it, though it affords the key to the view of God which this name reveals for the comfort of His creatures, necessarily fails, (for it is only a part of the wondrous record of " Elohim,") to express the overflowing riches of that unforsaking love, of which

---

[1] Heb. vi. 13.
[2] Heb. vi. 17, 18.
[3] Numb. xxiii. 19, 21.
[4] Rev. xxi. 3, 4.

this name, wherever it occurs in Scripture, is the ceaseless witness. Blessed be God for such a revelation. Shall we not pray for opened eyes, to understand all that is treasured up for us and for all creatures in " Elohim "? Shall we not bless Him who has said, " I will be to you a God "? Shall not every heart reply, " My Elohim, in Him will I trust "?[1]

[1] Psalm xci. 2.

2

LORD OR JEHOVAH

THE second name of God revealed in Holy Scripture, the name "Jehovah," which we translate "LORD," shews us qualities in God, which, though they are contained, can hardly be said to be expressed, in the first name, "Elohim."[1] For the name "Elohim," as we have seen, in its very import and by its plural form, spoke of One whose very Being involved a

---

[1] I may perhaps say here, for those who do not read Hebrew, that, in our Authorised Version, wherever we find the name "GOD" or "LORD" printed in capitals, the original is "Jehovah," (as in Gen. ii. 4, 5, 7, 8, &c. ; vi. 5, 6 ; xv. 2 ; xviii. 1, 13, 19, 22, 26 ; Ezek. ii. 4 ; iii. 11, 27 ; Obad. i. 1.) Wherever we find "God," (as in Gen. i. throughout, and in countless other passages,) it is "Elohim." Where we find "Lord," (as in Gen. xv. 2 ; xviii. 3, 27, 30, 31, 32 ; and constantly in the prophecies of Ezekiel,) it is "Adonai." Thus "LORD God" (in Gen. ii. 4, 5, 7, 8, and elsewhere,) is "Jehovah Elohim ; " while "Lord GOD" (in Gen. xv. 2, and Ezek. ii. 4, and elsewhere,) is "Adonai Jehovah." I may add that wherever the name "Jehovah" stands alone, (as in Gen. iv. 1, 3, 4, 6, 9, &c.) or is joined with "Elohim," (as in Gen. ii. 4, 5, 6, &c.,) it is always written in Hebrew with the vowel points of "Adonai : " where "Adonai" is joined to "Jehovah," (as in Gen. xv. 2 ; Ezek. ii. 4, &c.) "Jehovah" is written with the vowel points of "Elohim." For the Jews scrupulously avoided pronouncing the name "Jehovah," always reading "Adonai" for "Jehovah," except where "Adonai" is joined to "Jehovah," (as in Gen. xv. 2, and like passages,) in which case they read "Adonai Elohim."

covenant-relationship, which never could be broken.
" Jehovah " on the other hand, as we shall see, shews
One, who, being Love, is righteous also, and must
therefore judge evil, wherever it exists, and at whatever cost, whether to the creature or to the Creator.
Of course God is the same God, whether seen as
" Jehovah " or " Elohim ; " but " Elohim " gives us
only one view, blessed as that is, of God our Saviour.
We must know Him as " Jehovah " also, if we would
know ourselves, or what it costs the blessed God to
make us " partakers of His holiness." [1]

Let me try to shew more exactly what the difference between these two names is, and how the
One unchanging God, who in Himself is perfect
Love, may, as we apprehend Him, appear in very
different aspects or characters, either as Love or
Truth as " Elohim " or " Jehovah." St. John tells
us, " God is love." [2] This is what He absolutely is.
But in the expression of love we may see that love is
righteous also. As to His Being, God is Love, and
" Elohim " declares this. " Jehovah " reveals Him
as the Truth ; and Truth is not so much the Being
of God as the Expression of His Being. And as
apprehended by us these appear different, though in
themselves they are and must be one. Some may
not yet see this. But all I think will see how Love
must shew itself in truth and righteousness. Thus
the selfsame Love in its Being and in its Expression
may seem different. If we think of its Being, we

---

[1] Heb. xii. 10. [2] 1 John iv. 8, 16.

shall see a will which cannot change, because it
springs from and rests on being and relationship.
If we think of its Expression, we shall see how
variously it acts, and changes, or seems to change,
in virtue of certain qualities or conduct in the loved
one. A father's and still more a mother's unchanging
love illustrates the first, a love which cannot change,
spite of faults and failings in the loved one. This is
love in its Being. But the Expression of this love
varies in virtue of certain qualities in the beloved.
If therefore a child rebels, or a friend deceives, or if
a wife becomes unfaithful, there will be a breach of
love. You must, much as it may pain you, part
from them, and judge the evil; for if you do not, you
countenance their evil doings.

Now Holy Scripture presents us with both these
views of God. We have first the view of " Elohim,"
who, in virtue of His Being, in the might of love in
virtue of relationship, cares for and works on His
fallen creature, lost and fallen as it is, because it is
His creature, and He is Love, and therefore He can
never leave it nor forsake it. This is the view of
God so fully shewn us in the first chapter of the
Bible, and recognised and illustrated wherever we
read of " Elohim " and His doings. But there is the
second view, as to the Expression of love, namely,
love in its relation to certain qualities in the loved
one; and this it is which the name " Jehovah " so
wondrously reveals everywhere; shewing that God,
who is perfect love, is and must be a " God of

truth,"[1] and that in all truest love there must be righteousness. And with creatures such as we are the result is plain. If in God there is perfect love, such love in its expression must regard conduct and quality ; in other words, if there is in His love an element of righteousness, there may arise a breach between " Jehovah " and His creature ; and if the creature sin, there must be a breach and separation.

Here then we meet with the first, and perhaps the greatest, of these apparent antagonisms in God, of which, not Scripture only, but Nature also, is so full everywhere. God surely is love ; but if He loves only in virtue of quality, how can He love, what can He have to say to, sinners ? Must He not hate us for our evil ? On the other hand, if He only loves in virtue of relationship, what becomes of His righteousness, which must abhor and judge evil ? It seems a hard riddle. But without this apparent antagonism we could not know God. For to creatures in our present state, who only see things as they appear, the full truth, or things as they are, can only be taught by the union of apparent opposites. The view we first need of God is to see Him as " Elohim." With this name therefore God begins the revelation. But fully to know God, something more than this is needed. So long as only this view of Him is seen, there can be no proper knowledge either of righteousness or sin. For in " Elohim " what we chiefly see is One whose love

[1] Isa. lxv. 16.

works with and overcomes all, and whose will prevails, whatever the hindrances. More than this is needed : even the knowledge of righteousness and sin, and how our sin, which is the opposite of righteousness and love, wounds, not the creature only, but "Jehovah." All this comes out in the knowledge of the second name of God, which Holy Scripture reveals "to make the man of God perfect." [1]

This name "Jehovah," which thus supplements the primal name "Elohim," is first brought before us in the second and third chapters of the book of Genesis. In these chapters God is always "LORD God," in the Hebrew, "Jehovah Elohim," except where the serpent twice speaks of "God" to Eve,[2] and where the woman parleys with the serpent.[3] In both these cases, Eve and the serpent omit the name "Jehovah," and only speak of "God," as if they would shut their eyes to all except His covenant relationship :—"Yea, hath God said, Ye shall not eat of every tree of the garden?" and "God hath said, Ye shall not eat of it, nor touch it, lest ye die." All this is significant, as throwing light on the temptation. We are however now looking rather at the import of the name "Jehovah." And this name, like "Elohim," carries within itself its own meaning. It is formed of two tenses of the Hebrew verb, (Havah,) "to be," [4] and means, "One who is what He is," thus containing the substance of the well-known words to Moses,

---

[1] 2 Tim. iii. 17.   [2] Gen. iii. 1, 5.   [3] Gen. iii. 3.

[4] See Parkhurst's and Gesenius' *Lexicons*, under the word.

" I AM THAT I AM." [1] For these words, " I am that I am," are the expression of what God is. And this, if I err not, is the special and exact import of the name " Jehovah." " Jehovah " is the expression of God's being. And because He is true being, though He is love, He must be just and holy also, for evil is not true being, but the negation or privation of it.[2] If we do not see, we may yet believe, that " I AM THAT I AM " involves all this; for touching " Jehovah," Cherubim and Seraphim continually do cry, " Holy, Holy, Holy, LORD; " [3] and He says Himself, " Be holy, for I am holy." [4] " Jehovah " therefore is One, who " being what He is," " loves righteousness and hates iniquity," [5] and finds in all evil, if it exists, something antagonistic to His nature, which, because it is not true, must be opposed and judged. But this recognition of something to which He is opposed, and which opposes Him, opens a depth which is never seen until we know " Jehovah." What this possibility of a will antagonistic to His own involves, not to the creature only, but to " Jehovah," is here told as only God could tell it. It

---

[1] Exod. iii. 14.

[2] The great answer of the early Church to the Manichæan error always was, that evil is τὸ μὴ ὄν, that is, *not true being* ; therefore not eternal. God is true being ; ὁ ὤν. So Athanasius, *Orat. c. Gentes*, c. 4 and 6 ; Basil, *Hom.* "Quod Deus non est auctor malorum," c. 5 ; Gregory of Nyssa, *Orat. Catech.* c. 28 ; and Augustine, *De Moribus Manich.* lib. ii. § 2 and 3, and *Confess.* lib. vii. c. 12.

[3] Isa. vi. 2, 3 ; and Rev. iv. 8.   [4] Lev. xi. 44, 45.

[5] Psalm xlv. 7.

is a wondrous vision, but it is most distinctly presented
wherever " Jehovah " shews Himself; not least in
those early chapters of Holy Scripture where this
name is first revealed to us.

Let us then look more closely at the second and
third chapters of Genesis. Man as well as God are
seen here in an aspect very different to that which is
set before us in the first chapter. There after the
" waters " and the " earth " by the Word of God had
" brought forth the moving creatures which had life,"—
literally " the moving creatures which have a living
soul," [1]—" God created man in His own image,"
and " set him to have dominion over the fish of the
sea, and the fowl of the air, and over all cattle, and
over every creeping thing that creepeth upon the
earth." [2] But in the second chapter, where " Jehovah "
appears, man is shewn as " formed of the dust of the
ground,"[3] then there is " breathed into his nostrils
the breath of lives,[4] and man became, (what the
creatures had been before him,) a living soul." [5] This

---

[1] Heb. נפש חיה; literally translated "living soul," in the
margin of the Authorised Version, vv. 20 and 30.

[2] Gen. i. 26, 28.

[3] Three different words,—namely ברא " *created* ;" עשה,
' *made* ; " and יצר, " *formed*,"—are used, surely not without a purpose, as to God's work, in Gen. i. and ii. The first, probably connected with בר, " *a son*," is to " create," or " generate : " the
second is to " make " out of existing materials : the third is to
" mould " or " form," as a potter moulds the clay. All these three
words occur in one verse, in Isa. xliii. 7 :—" I have *created* him
for my glory   have *formed* him ; yea, I have *made* him.

[4] Plural in he Hebrew : נשמת חיים.

[5] Gen. ii. 7. The word here translated, " *living soul* " is

is not seen until "Jehovah" is revealed. Then, having "become a living soul," man so "formed" is at once put under law. Instead of "God blessed him," as in the first chapter,[1] we have now, "Jehovah God commanded the man."[2] Can we forget here the Apostle's words, "The law is not made for a righteous man"?[3] After which "every beast and fowl is brought to man, to see what he would call them;" but among them all "for Adam there was not found a help meet for him." What had taken place I do not fully know, but this at least is certain, that whereas, when "God created man in His own image," He said that "all was very good,"[4] "Jehovah Elohim" now first says, "It is not good;"[5] and the result is, that the man is thrown into "a deep sleep," —a sleep which the Church has always viewed as figuring the cross and death of Christ,[6] for indeed all sleep is the brother of death,—after which the man originally made in God's image, is divided, the woman taken out of the man, so that we have division where till now there had been oneness.

---

exactly the same as that used respecting the beasts, in Gen. i. 20, 30. The text describes the genesis of what St. Paul calls the "natural" (or psychical) man. See 1 Cor. xv. 44-46; and 1 Cor. ii. 14. If I err not, Gen. i. 27 speaks of the creation of the "spiritual" man.

[1] Gen. i. 28. [2] Gen. ii. 16, 17.
[3] 1 Tim. i. 9. [4] Gen. i. 31.
[5] Gen. ii. 18.

[6] So Augustine, in Psalm cxxvii. (E. V. cxxviii.,) § 11; and in Psalm cxxvi. (E. V. cxxvii.) § 7. This interpretation is common to nearly all the Fathers.

So much as to the altered view here given of man. What is shewn of " Jehovah " is, if possible, even more significant. Every word presents Him as One who marks quality and looks for righteousness. Even in Paradise He has, beside the " tree of life," the " tree of the knowledge of good and evil " also,[1] thus from the very beginning calling attention to the difference between these. Then, as we have already seen, He puts man under law, saying both " Thou shalt," and " Thou shalt not," [2] with a warning and threat that disobedience must surely bring judgment. And then, when man disobeys, " Jehovah" pronounces judgment, sending him forth from Eden to eat bread by the sweat of his brow, until he return unto the ground from whence he was taken ; [3] yet not without hope, for in the very judgment there is a promise of deliverance :—" The seed of the woman shall bruise the serpent's head." [4] But the vision throughout is of One whose love is in virtue of quality ; whose will therefore can be obeyed or crossed, and whose will actually is crossed, by His creatures, though not with impunity ; and who therefore, (if one may say so,) is subject to His creature's acceptance and rejection,—for He may have His Paradise stripped and emptied of its heir,—and so may be affected by the destructions which sin brings with it into God's creation. Oh, what a picture these early chapters of Genesis give us of " Jehovah." He makes for the man whom He

---

[1] Gen. ii. 9.
[2] Gen. ii. 16, 17.
[3] Gen. iii. 17–19.
[4] Gen. iii. 15.

has formed a Paradise, with every tree that is
pleasant to the sight and good for food. He puts
him there to walk in converse with Himself. Because
He is Himself holy, He gives man a commandment,
which is holy, just and good. And the serpent's word
is preferred to " Jehovah's." So Paradise is emptied
of its heir : " Jehovah's " work is marred : His will
is crossed : His holy law is broken.

Such is the first record we have of " Jehovah,"
every detail of which marks the view of God
which this name reveals everywhere. All that Holy
Scripture further records respecting this name only
emphasizes its contrast to " Elohim," and reveals
more fully those characteristics of " Jehovah " which
the story of the Fall brings out so clearly. Take the
fourth and fifth chapters of Genesis as an example,
the former of which speaks only of " Jehovah," except where Eve says something of " another seed ; "[1]
the latter no less exclusively of " Elohim." In the
former we have the record of the woman's seed :
in the latter, the generations of the Son of Man.
Throughout the former we are told of the woman
" conceiving," and then of her varied seed, which is
set before us as marked by varying tastes and qualities. Thus we read, " Adam knew his wife, and she
conceived and bare Cain ; and she again bare his
brother Abel. And Abel was a keeper of sheep, and
Cain a tiller of the ground. . . . And Cain knew his
wife, and she conceived and bare Enoch, and he

[1] See verse 25.

builded a city. And unto Enoch was born Irad. . . . And Lamech took two wives, Adah and Zillah; and Adah bare Jabal: he was the father of such as dwell in tents: and his brother's name was Jubal: he was the father of all such as handle the harp and organ. And Zillah, she also bare Tubal-Cain, an instructor of every artificer in brass and iron."[1] All this variety of quality in the woman's seed, in strictest conformity with the name under which it is revealed, is set before us under "Jehovah," who loves in virtue of quality, and who therefore "has respect to one," while to another He "has not respect;"[2] who accepts one, while He judges and rejects another. How entirely different is the other record, in the fifth chapter, where we have the generations of the Son of Man, under "Elohim," where no reference is made to quality, but only to relationship; the one great fact, repeated generation after generation, being that the man "begat sons and daughters," and "lived" so long, and then "died."[3] Every word is distinctive and significant. It is thus also in the judgment of the Antediluvian world: how marked is the revelation respecting "Jehovah." We read, "And Jehovah saw that the wickedness of man was great in the earth. And Jehovah said, My Spirit shall not always strive with man; yet his days shall be a hundred and twenty years. And Jehovah said, I will destroy man whom I have created . . . and it repented Him that He

---

[1] Gen. iv. 1-22.   [2] Gen. iv. 4, 5.
[3] Gen. v. 4, 7, 10, 13, &c.

had made man." What is all this in substance but
a repetition of what we saw in Eden? Jehovah is
righteous: He must judge evil. But the sin of
man crosses and grieves Him. If His creatures
suffer, He too suffers. So it is added, "And it
repented Jehovah that He had made man, and
it grieved Him at His heart."[1]   Need I shew
how all this differs from the vision of "Elohim"?
"Jehovah" loves righteousness. If sin come into
His creation, it crosses Him, and therefore must be
judged.

I cannot go into all the details, yet I may perhaps
notice in the record of the Flood, how the names
"Elohim" and "Jehovah" are again and again inter-
changed in a way which cannot but strike a thought-
ful reader. For instance, in Genesis vi. 8, we read,
that "Noah found grace in the eyes of Jehovah,"
while in the very next verse it is written, that "Noah
walked with Elohim." For "Jehovah" is the "Holy,
Holy, Holy, Lord," before whom even the heavenly
cherubim "veil their faces:"[2] He Himself says, "No
man can see my face and live:"[3] while in "Elohim" the
revelation is of a love in virtue of relationship. Noah
therefore and Enoch may "walk with Elohim, and
beget sons and daughters;"[4] but "Noah found grace
in the eyes of Jehovah," for "Noah was a just man and
perfect in his generations."[5]   Again, in Genesis vi. 5,

---

[1] Gen. vi. 3, 5, 6, 7.   [2] Isa. vi. 2.

[3] Exod. xxxiii. 20.   [4] Gen. v. 22.

[5] Gen. vi. 8, 9.

we read, " Jehovah saw the wickedness of man, that
it was great upon the earth. . . . And Jehovah said,
I will destroy man whom I have created ; " while only
a few verses later,[1] we read, " And Elohim saw the
earth, and behold it was corrupt, for all flesh had
corrupted his way. And Elohim said, I will destroy
them with the earth : make thee an ark of gopher
wood; for with thee will I establish my covenant."
Here the righteous " Jehovah " says only, " I will destroy ; " while when " Elohim " utters the same words,
He adds directions as to " the Ark," and a promise as
to the establishment of His " covenant." Every word
is characteristic. So again, in Genesis vi. 22, we
read, " Thus did Noah according to all that Elohim
commanded him ; " while in chapter vii. 5, we have,
" And Noah did according to all that Jehovah
commanded him." But here again the context shews
the reason for the change of name. For in " Elohim's "
command only " two of every living thing were to be
taken into the ark," [2] for these " two " would continue
the race, according to the will of Him who loves in
virtue of relationship. " Jehovah's " added command
is, " Of every clean beast thou shalt take to thee by
sevens," [3] for " Jehovah " the truth-requiring God
looks for sacrifices. Therefore after the flood, " Of
every clean beast Noah offered burnt-offerings to
Jehovah," [4] when righteous judgment had purged the
earth of its pollution.

---

[1] Gen. vi. 12–18.
[3] Chap. vii. 2.

[2] Chap. vi. 19.
[4] Chap. viii. 20.

But Israel, to whom this name was especially revealed, is the great illustration of what " Jehovah " really is, though here, as in every revelation, eyes are needed to see, and ears to hear, what Holy Scripture sets before us. The revelation however is most distinct, whether in the Law, the Prophets, or the Psalms. Hear first the Law. In it " Jehovah " always speaks as the One who loves righteousness, and requires His own likeness in His people :—" Hear, O Israel, Jehovah our God is one Jehovah. And thou shalt love Jehovah thy God with all thy heart, and with all thy soul, and with all thy might; "[1] that is, Thou shalt be like the LORD thy God. Every word is a demand for a love like " Jehovah's " own, and testifies of a requirement of righteousness and love in the beloved. This is the thought all through the Law, in its threatenings and promises as much as in its commandments. Therefore we read again, " And it shall come to pass, if ye shall hearken diligently to my commandments, to love Jehovah your God, and to serve Him with all your heart, that I will give you the rain of your land in due season, that thou mayest gather in thy corn and wine and oil."[2] " But if ye will not obey the voice of Jehovah, but rebel against His commandments, then shall the hand of Jehovah be against you, as it was against your fathers."[3] Indeed the great offence of Israel, after being redeemed by " Jehovah," " to be a nation

---

[1] Deut. vi. 4, 5. See too Deut. x. 12 ; and Josh. xxii. 5.

[2] Deut. xi. 13.   [3] 1 Sam. xii. 15.

of priests and a holy nation to Jehovah,"[1] is that
they are not a holy people, and that they do not
walk as the people of " Jehovah," the truth-requiring
God.[2] And all that is enjoined, whether as to " the
offerings of the LORD," or, "the priests of the LORD,"or,
" the temple of the LORD," or, " the altar or table of the
LORD," in a word all the appointed service of "Jehovah," expresses requirement,—a requirement which
is for our good, yet a requirement to be satisfied, and
which calls for ceaseless sacrifices, even to the pouring
out of life, and of giving our best with gladness to Him.
Sacrifice therefore even unto death,—a shedding of
blood, that is a pouring out of life, in His service,
in the sweet-savour offerings as much as in the sin
and trespass offerings,—very specially marks the worship of Jehovah. His people must be holy :—" Ye
shall be holy, for I, Jehovah your God, am holy."[3]
And again, " I am Jehovah your God. Ye shall
therefore sanctify yourselves, for I am holy."[4]

If we grasp, even in measure, the meaning of
this name, " Jehovah," we may better understand
what " Elohim " said to Moses, " I am Jehovah,
and I appeared unto Abraham, unto Isaac, and unto
Jacob, by the name God Almighty ; but by my name
Jehovah was I not known to them."[5] God had
always been " Jehovah," but in the character which
this name declares, that is, as the God whose love
would be in virtue of certain qualities, even His

---

[1] Exod. xix. 6.   [2] Amos iii. 2.   [3] Lev. xix. 2.
[4] Lev. xx. 24, 26.   [5] Exod. vi. 2.

elect, Abraham, Isaac, and Jacob, had not as yet known Him. To them He had been known rather as "Elohim," that is, in covenant, or as "El Shaddai," that is, God Almighty. Not until the redemption out of Egypt, when He gave the law, and said, "Be ye holy, for I am holy," was the full import of the name "Jehovah" revealed to Israel. Eve had known it,[1] for she knew judgment. Noah too knew it,[2] for he had seen the Flood. But the life of faith, and sonship, and service, (and Abraham, Isaac, and Jacob, figure these,[3]) often goes far before it fully knows "Jehovah."

So much as to the revelation of "Jehovah" under the Law. But the same love of quality is no less seen in what the Prophets witness of Him :—" If a man be just, and do that which is lawful and right, and hath walked in my statutes and kept my judgments, he is just, he shall surely live, saith the Lord Jehovah, . . . but he that doeth not any of these duties, . . . he shall surely die ; his blood shall be upon him." [4] This is the ceaseless witness of the "prophets of Jehovah." [5] They cry aloud and spare not, lifting up their voices like a trumpet, to shew Jehovah's people their transgression, and the house of Jacob their sins ; [6] saying, "I have loved you with an everlasting love ; " [7] and yet "the soul that sinneth, it shall die." [8] For "I, Jehovah thy God,

---

[1] Gen. iv. 1.   [2] Gen. ix. 26.

[3] See *Types of Genesis*, pp. 159, 160.

[4] Ezek. xviii. 5, 9, 11, 12.

[5] 1 Sam. iii. 20 ; 1 Kings xxii. 7 ; 2 Chron. xxviii. 9.

[6] Isa. lviii. 1.   [7] Jer. xxxi. 3.   [8] Ezek. xviii. 4, 20.

am a jealous God, visiting the iniquity of the fathers
upon the children, unto the third and fourth generation of them that hate me, and shewing mercy unto
thousands of them that love me and keep my commandments." [1] This testimony never changes. The
Psalms are full of it :—" Upon the wicked, Jehovah
shall rain snares, fire and brimstone, and an hor-
rible tempest : this shall be the portion of their cup.
For the righteous Jehovah loveth righteousness, His
countenance doth behold the upright." [2]

And yet with Israel, even as in Eden, and with
the world before the Flood, while He most inflexibly
inflicts judgment, we are shewn again and again,
what so few think of, that sin grieves and wounds
" Jehovah," and that He also suffers, if His people
are disobedient. He Himself is pained by the destructions which sin must bring with it. Unless we
see this, we do not know " Jehovah." But here, as
throughout the whole record of " Jehovah," the testimony is most clear. Again and again, when Israel
sinned, " the anger of Jehovah was kindled against
His people, and Jehovah sold them into the hands of
their enemies ; " but it is not Israel only that is " sore
distressed ; " for of " Jehovah " also it is written,
" And His soul was grieved for the misery of Israel." [3]
So, again the Prophet declares, " Behold, I am pressed
under you, as a cart is pressed that is full of sheaves ; " [4]
that is, He is pressed and burdened, and goes groan-

---

[1] Exod. xx. 5.
[2] Psalm xi. 7.
[3] Judges x. 6, 7, 9, 16.
[4] Amos ii. 13.

ing. So again the Psalmist says, " Forty years long was I grieved with this generation in the wilderness." [1] " In all their afflictions He was afflicted." [2] Who can measure the anguish of His words :—" How shall I give thee up, Ephraim ? how shall I deliver thee, Israel ? how shall I make thee as Admah? how shall I set thee as Zeboim ? My heart is turned within me, my repentings are kindled together." [3]

We are slow to see all this. And yet if Jesus Christ really reveals " Jehovah : " if He is indeed " the brightness of His glory, and the express image of His person : " [4] if He is, as the Apostle says, " the image of the invisible God : " [5] then His cross and sufferings shew, not only that sin brings death and sorrow upon men, but (if we may say it) sorrow and trouble also on " Jehovah." Christ's cross is the witness of " Jehovah's " cross, though by His cross He conquers all. " Surely He hath borne our griefs." [6] Was it no grief to Him that His people rejected Him ? " When He was come near and beheld the city, He wept over it." [7] Was He not crossed ? He makes a feast, and none will come but those who are compelled. He says, " Come, for all things are now ready ; and they all with one consent began to make excuse." [8] Can we misunderstand His oft repeated words :—" How often would I have

Psalm xcv. 10.   [2] Isa. lxiii. 9.

Hos. xi. 8.   [4] Heb. i. 3.

Col. i. 15.   [6] Isa. liii. 4.   [7] St. Luke xix. 41.

Matt. xxii. 4, 5; St. Luke xiv. 16–18.

gathered you, and ye would not "? [1] His complaint is, " All the day long have I stretched forth my hands to a disobedient and gainsaying people." [2] For a time at least His will is crossed. Oh wonder of all wonders! " Jehovah " suffers as only righteous Love can suffer.

But there is more even than this in the revelation of " Jehovah," though the crowning glory of the revelation is only yet dimly seen by many of His people. Not only is He the God who requires righteousness; not only is He Himself affected by the destructions which sin has brought upon His creature; but still more, blessed be His name, His righteousness is not fully declared until He makes His creatures righteous with His own righteousness. What we first see in Him is law, and that, because He is righteous, He must condemn evil. But we should greatly err if we therefore concluded that this could be the end, for the new covenant of grace is His also. [3] It is " Jehovah " who says, " This is the covenant that I will make after those days,"— (that is after law has done its work of condemnation,) —" I will put my law into their mind, and will write it in their hearts, and I will be to them a God, and they shall be to me a people." Righteousness is not complete, if it only judges and condemns; for the devil also can condemn. The highest righteousness,

---

[1] St. Matt. xxiii. 37 ; St. Luke xiii. 34.

[2] Isa. lxv. 2 ; Rom. x. 21.

[3] Jer. xxxi. 31–34; Heb. viii. 8–12.

while it judges sin, can never rest until it also makes
the sinner righteous. The saints have always felt
this, and that God's righteousness is for them, not
against them; saying, " I know, O Jehovah, that
thy judgments are right, and that in very faithfulness thou hast afflicted me." [1]   " Quicken me, O
Jehovah, for thy name's sake : for thy righteousness
sake bring my soul out of trouble." [2]   " In thy name
shall thy people rejoice all the day, and in thy
righteousness shall they be exalted." [3]   Because He
is righteous, evil must be judged : the evil-doer must
be punished. But the evil being thus judged, and
the sinner condemned, the righteous God is no less
righteous,—rather He is yet more righteous,—in
making the judged creature a " partaker of His
holiness." [4]   Therefore St. Paul calls the Gospel
" the ministration of righteousness, which exceeds
in glory," even while he declares that the law, or
" ministration of condemnation," has its own, though
an inferior, " glory." [5]   Therefore he says again, that
our " being made righteous freely by His grace " is
" to declare God's righteousness." [6]   Thus, though
" sin reigns unto death, grace no less reigns through
righteousness unto eternal life, by Jesus Christ our
Lord." [7]   For " Jehovah " is not content to be
righteous Himself.   Unlike the Pharisee, who thanks
God that " he is not as other men," [8]   " Jehovah "

---

[1] Psalm cxix. 75.   [2] Psalm cxliii. 11.
[3] Psalm lxxxix. 15, 16.   [4] Heb. xii. 10.
    2 Cor. iii. 7–9.   [6] Rom. iii. 24, 25.
[7] Rom. v. 21.   [8] St. Luke xviii. 11.

will have the creature made like Himself, by coming into its place, and making it sharer in His own righteousness. In a word, " He is just, and (therefore) the justifier." [1] " He leadeth me in paths of righteousness for His name's sake." [2] For to sum up all, as the Prophet says, " This is the name whereby He shall be called, The LORD, that is, Jehovah, our righteousness." [3] This, and nothing less, is " the end of the LORD." [4] He condemns to justify; He kills to make alive; that is to make the creature righteous as He is righteous. [5] But, as I have said, there are not a few from whom this part of the revelation of " Jehovah " is more or less hidden. Even men of faith, like Abram, do not see it for awhile. It comes out after the name " El Shaddai," that is " God Almighty," is revealed, and the man of faith is changed from Abram into Abraham.

Such is a brief outline of the revelation of " Jehovah." When it is seen in its completeness, it shews, what we so slowly learn, that God's love of righteousness is for us, as much as the love which springs from, and is in virtue of, relationship : nay more, that even the judgment and the curse involve a blessing; in other words, that " Jehovah " is a Saviour as truly as " Elohim." [6] It shews too how

---

[1] Rom. iii. 26. [2] Psalm xxiii. 3.
[3] Jer. xxiii. 6. [4] St. James v. 11.
[5] The whole of Scripture is full of this thought. See Psalm lxxxv. 16–18; cxviii. 18–20 ; Isa. xxvi. 9.
[6] How mysterious are Jehovah's ways. " Neither to Adam nor

the names of God, like the Four Gospels, overlap
each other, each more or less containing something
of that unutterable love, the fulness of which can
only be expressed from stage to stage in successive
revelations as we can bear it. Certainly in " Elohim's "
dividing the light from the darkness, and the waters
below from the waters above, and the fruitful earth
from the salt and barren waters,[1] we see something
of that discriminating love which is characteristic of
" Jehovah," though, as we have seen, the revelation
in " Elohim " is a love in virtue of relationship. So
in " Jehovah," while this name expresses true being,
and reveals One, who, because He is the Truth, must
condemn all evil and unrighteousness, we may yet
see, even in His judgments to make His creatures like
Himself, tokens of the unforsaking love of which
Elohim is the witness; while in His giving His own
nature and righteousness to His creatures we have
still further glimpses of that vision which the following name " El Shaddai," or " Almighty," more distinctly declares to us. For God's perfections are
inseparable. All really are in all, though we learn
them by degrees, and as our need calls for the growing revelation.

I will only add here, that when " Jehovah " is
first revealed, as in the second and third chapters of

---

to Eve was there one word of comfort spoken. The only hint of
such a thing was given in the act of cursing the serpent. The
curse involved the blessing."—*The Eternal Purpose of God*, by
A. L. Newton, p. 10.

[1] Gen. i. 4, 6, 9.

Genesis, His primal name, " Elohim," is always added
also, except, as we have seen, where the woman or
the serpent speak, who speak only of " Elohim."
Every act and word is of " Jehovah Elohim ; " to shew
that, though He is all that " Jehovah " expresses,
One who is righteous and must judge sin, He never
ceases to be " Elohim " also, who loves unforsakingly,
because He loves in virtue of relationship ; that
therefore to the very end, even if man falls, there is
" hope for him in God," [1] who says, " There is no
Elohim besides me : look unto me, and be ye saved,
all the ends of the earth, for I am God, and there is
none else ; " who yet says, in the same breath, " I am
Jehovah, a just God and a Saviour ; " and again,
" Surely shall one say, In Jehovah have I righteousness and strength. . . . In Jehovah shall all the
seed of Israel be justified and shall glory." [2] The
names are often intermingled, but always with a
purpose, to bring out something distinctive in our
God, the knowledge of which adds to His people's
strength or gladness. " Blessed are the people who
know the joyful sound : they shall walk, O Jehovah,
in the light of thy countenance. In thy name shall
they rejoice all the day, and in thy righteousness
shall they be exalted." [3] Shall we not then pray
with Moses, " I beseech thee, shew me thy glory,"
when, as with Moses, " Jehovah passes before us,"
and proclaims His name,—" Jehovah, the LORD God,

---

[1] Psalm iii. 2 ; xlii. 11.   [2] Isa. xlv. 21, 25.

[3] Psalm lxxxix. 15, 16.

merciful and gracious, long suffering, and abundant in goodness and truth, keeping mercy for thousands, forgiving iniquity and transgression and sin, and that will by no means clear the guilty." [1]   Shall we not say with the Psalmist, " I will sing unto the LORD as long as I live : " " I will say of Jehovah, He is my refuge." [2]

---

[1] Exod. xxxiii. 18; and xxxiv. 6, 7.

[2] Psalm civ. 33 ; and xci. 2.

3

GOD ALMIGHTY OR EL SHADDAI

WE have already seen how the revelation of the
first two names of God, "Elohim" and "Jehovah,"
involves what looks like an antagonism. "Elohim"
is One who is in covenant-relationship, and loves in
virtue of relationship; who therefore carries on His
new creation work accordingly to His own purpose,
till all is very good. "Jehovah," on the other hand,
reveals true being; One therefore who must be
opposed to all that is false and evil, that is, to all
that is not true being; and who must judge it,
because His will is crossed by evil, even though He
Himself suffers with His creatures in the judgment.
We cannot deny that there is something which looks
like a contradiction here, between a God who carries
out His purpose according to His will, and One whose
heart is grieved and whose will is crossed by the disobedience of the creature. But Holy Scripture does
not shrink from repeating this apparent contradiction.
We see it in the seeming opposition between the truth
of God's free grace and man's free will, and in the no
less seeming contradiction that our Lord's sacrifice
and death was at the same moment both a sweet-

savour and a non-sweet-savour offering. How, it has been asked, can it be true that all is of God's grace; "not of him that willeth, nor of him that runneth, but of God that sheweth mercy;" [1] and yet that God can say, "Ye will not come unto me, that ye might have life;" [2] "How often would I have gathered you, and ye would not"? [3] How is it possible that our Lord's sacrifice, even unto death, could have been voluntarily offered by Him, as the most perfect freewill offering of love, and therefore most acceptable to God, as a sweet savour upon His altar; and yet that at the same time it should be penal, the divinely required and necessary vindication of a broken law? Yet Holy Scripture distinctly teaches that Christ's sacrifice has both these aspects; and, as we pass from things as they appear to things as they are, we see that no sacrifice can be perfect, unless it is at the same time both voluntary and involuntary. So as to God Himself. It is only in the union of apparent opposites, (as I have already said,) that we can get even glimpses of His unmeasured and immeasurable fulness. To contend therefore only for one view or side of truth against another, simply because under the limitations of our present nature we cannot at once logically reconcile the two, is to shut ourselves out from that more perfect knowledge to which God leads us by varied revelations. But how many are thus "straitening themselves," [4] losing thereby the

---

[1] Rom. ix. 16.

[2] St. John v. 40.

[3] St. Matt. xxiii. 37.

[4] 2 Cor. vi. 12, 13.

fulness of the light, which the acceptance of every ray of His truth, however much one may seem to differ from another, must always bring with it.

And both saints and sinners may err in this way, through one-sided views of truth. On the one hand careless souls, with their vague hope of some future salvation, on the ground that God is merciful and can " never leave us nor forsake us," shut their eyes to the no less certain fact that He is righteous, and must judge, not all evil only, but evildoers also, to the uttermost. On the other, those who have learnt that God is righteous, and that His will is crossed by sin, which He must judge, conclude that, because it is now so crossed, it will be crossed for ever, and that, because He is righteous, though He desires to save all, He must for ever lose a portion of His creatures. If these careless souls could only see that their thought ignores God's holiness, and that all evil sooner or later must be judged, because the LORD is righteous, they could hardly live as they do in their present carelessness, but would judge themselves, that they might not be judged of the LORD. On the other hand, if those who think of God as just, and that He must condemn evil, could but go on to know the LORD as He is revealed under the names " Almighty " and " Most High," they would see how their view of " Jehovah " yet lacks something, and that there are powers in the " Almighty " and the " Most High," which cannot permit God to be crossed for ever, but which, first in His elect, and then by them, can and must accomplish His will, that all men should be saved, and should come to a knowledge of the truth.[1]

For the third and fourth names under which God is revealed in Holy Scripture, the name " Almighty," by which He revealed Himself to Abram, the man of faith, and the name " Most High," by which He was known to the Canaanite King, Melchisedek, if we can read them aright, give God's solution of the seeming contradiction, first, to the elect, and then to those who are as far off as the Canaanite. But to know " El Shaddai," we must be like him to whom this name was first revealed, and, even if we are such, there are many stages to be trodden before this revelation is vouchsafed to us. For the man of faith " gets him out of his country," and then " from his kindred and his father's house," and has some experience of Canaan, and has gone down thence to Egypt, and has denied Sarai, and is yet without the promised seed, though he has sought it by Hagar, that is by law, and by his own energy,[2] before he hears the words, " I am God Almighty," and learns in self-judgment how the strength of God is made perfect in our weakness. If we know nothing of this path, there may be things yet beyond us in the revelation of " El Shaddai," even though we may be Abrams, that is men of faith, who seek to be obedient. But a time comes when the name is known, when we learn, not in word but deed, how the self-willed crea-

---

[1] 1 Tim. ii. 4-6.   [2] See Gen. xii. 1, 5, 11, 12; and Gal. iv. 24.

ture can be blessed, and " Jehovah's " will, crossed by man's sin, shall henceforth by grace be crossed no more. The LORD Himself, the " Almighty," help me, while I try to open what may be opened here respecting this name, " El Shaddai," or " Almighty."

And, first, to say what this name, " Almighty," does *not* mean, (for there may be some misapprehensions respecting this,) that we may better see what it does mean.

" Almighty " is supposed by some to mean One who has the power to do anything and everything. But such an idea of Almightiness is not that which Holy Scripture presents to us. Holy Scripture says that God is Truth [1] and Love.[2] As the true and righteous God, the very Truth, He " cannot lie." [3] He " *cannot*." Does this " cannot " limit His Almightiness ? Would He be more Almighty, if He could lie ? Certainly not. Falsehood is weakness. Almightiness therefore is not the power of doing anything or everything. Almightiness is the power to carry out the will of a Divine nature. It is no part of God's nature to be false or lie. It is therefore no limiting of His Almightiness to say, He " cannot lie."

But God is also Love. His will is to bless all.[4] Would it be any proof of His Almightiness, if, instead of being able to save and bless His creatures, He could only punish and destroy them ? Take an

---

[1] Isa. lxv. 16.   [2] 1 St. John iv. 8.
[3] Tit. i. 2 ; Numb. xxiii. 19.   [4] 1 Tim. ii. 4 ; 2 St. Pet. iii. 9.

illustration. Suppose a sculptor, who desired to form an image of himself out of some material, whether of wood, or stone, or metal. Would it be any proof of his power as a sculptor, if, because the stone, or wood, or metal, were hard to work on, he dashed his image all to pieces? Would such an act shew his ability? Quite the reverse. And so with God. To be " Almighty," He must be able to carry out His own will and purpose to the uttermost. And this will is to save His creatures, and to restore and re-form His image in them. If He cannot do this, and " turn the hearts of the disobedient to the wisdom of the just," [1] He is not able to fulfil the desire of His nature, and so would not be Almighty. I say, " *If* He cannot do this." Thank God, " He is able to subdue all things unto Himself." [2] And, because He is Love, to " subdue all things to Himself " is to subdue all things to Love.

Now this third name, " God Almighty," in the Hebrew " El Shaddai," taken in connexion with the circumstances under which it was revealed to the man of faith, opens the secret how He does this.

The name itself says not a little. " El," which is so often and rightly translated " God," primarily means " might," or " power," and is used in this sense in not a few passages of Holy Scripture. So Laban says, " It is in the *power* (El) of my hand to do you hurt." [3] So again Moses, foretelling the judgments which should come on Israel, for their sins,

---

[1] St. Luke i. 17.　　[2] Phil. iii. 21.　　[3] Gen. xxxi. 29.

says, " Thy sons and thy daughters shall be given
to another people, . . . and there shall be no *might*
(El) in thine hand." [1] Where the word is applied to
the One true God, as it continually is, it always
assumes His power. So David says, " It is El that
girdeth me with strength ; " [2] and again, " Thou art
the El, that doest wonders." [3] When it is applied to

---

[1] Deut. xxviii. 32. For further examples of this use of " El,"
see Neh. v. 5, where we read, " Some of our daughters are brought
into bondage, neither is it in our *power* (El) to redeem them."
So too Prov. iii. 27 :—" Withhold not good from them to whom it
is due, when it is in the *power* (El) of thine hand to do it ; " and
again in Micah ii. 1 :—" They practise evil, because it is in the
power (El) of their hand." Parkhurst's note on the root idea of
this word, " El " as expressing *Interposition* or *Intervention*, even
when applied, as it so constantly is, to God, is well worth turning
to. See his *Lexicon*, under the word אֵל.

[2] Psalm xviii. 32.

[3] Psalm lxxvii. 14. To a mere English reader there will
always be a difficulty in knowing whether the name " God " in
our English version is " Elohim " or " El " in the original. For
both these names have been alike translated " God," while there
is an important difference in their signification. When I state
again that " Elohim " is translated " God " about two thousand
two hundred and fifty times, and that " El " is also translated
by the same word, " God," no less than two hundred and twenty-
five times in our Authorised Version of the Old Testament, and
that there is nothing in our translation to mark the difference
between these two names, it will at once be evident that it must
be impossible for a mere English reader to know whether some
given passage, where the name " God " occurs in our version,
speaks of " El " or of " Elohim." If a Revised Version of the
Old Testament is ever issued by authority, it would surely be
well in some way to mark where the original reads " El," and
where it is " Elohim." See further as illustrating this name " El,"
Deut. iii. 24 ; Psalm lxviii. 35 ; lxxviii. 19 ; lxxix. 7 ; Neh. ix. 32 ;
Job xxxvi. 5, 26 ; xl. 9 ; Isa. xl. 18 ; xlvi. 9 ; &c.

angels or men, the same idea of power is always present in it;[1] as also when it is used of lower creatures, such as "Behemoth," who in virtue of his power is called, "chief of the ways of El,"[2] or of the "great mountains" or "goodly cedars," which are called "mountains of El," or "cedars of El," because they surpass others in magnificence.[3] The thought expressed in the name "Shaddai" is different,[4] though it also describes power; but it is the power, not of violence, but of all-bountifulness. "Shaddai" primarily means "*Breasted*," being formed directly from the Hebrew word "*Shad*," that is, "*the breast*," or, more exactly, a "*woman's breast*."[5] Parkhurst thus explains the name :—"Shaddai, one of the Divine titles, meaning '*The Pourer or Shedder forth*,' that is, of blessings, temporal and spiritual." But inasmuch as the pourings forth even of the breast, if not properly received, may choke a child; as the rain from heaven, if not drunk in by the earth, may form torrents, and cause ruin and destruction ; the same word came to have another meaning, namely to *sweep away* or *make desolate*;[6] and this thought also

---

[1] Psalm xxix. 1 ; lxxxii. 1 ; lxxxix. 6.   [2] Job xl. 19.

[3] Psalm xxxvi. 6 ; and lxxx. 10.   [4] Heb. שׁדי.

[5] Heb. שׁד. See Gen. xlix. 25; Job iii. 12; Psalm xxii. 9; Cant. i. 13; iv. 5; vii. 3, 7, 8; viii. 1, 8, 18; Isa. xxviii. 9; Lam. iv. 3; Ezek. vi. 7 ; and xxiii. 3, and other passages ; in all which the word translated "breasts" is "Shad," the direct root of "Shaddai." Our English word to "shed" is said by some to come from the same root, which can be traced also in Sanscrit.

[6] For instances of this secondary sense of שׁד see Job v. 22;

may be connected with the name "Shaddai," for
blessings and gifts misused become curses. The
kindred name, " Sheddim," [1] referred to as objects of
idolatrous worship in other parts of Scripture, (and
in our Authorised Version translated " devils," [2]) describes " the many-breasted idols, representing the
genial powers of nature," which were " worshipped
among the heathen, as givers of rain, and pourers
forth of fruits and increase." [3] " El Shaddai " is the
true Giver of His own life, of whom these heathen
" Sheddim " were the idolatrous perversion. In this
name the men of faith have ever trusted, of His
fulness to receive grace for grace.

If this is seen, I need hardly explain how this
title, the " Breasted," or the " Pourer-forth," came
to mean " Almighty." Mothers at least will understand it. A babe is crying,—restless. Nothing can
quiet it. Yes : the breast can. A babe is pining,—
starving. Its life is going out. It cannot take
man's proper food : it will die. No : the breast can
give it fresh life, and nourish it. By her breast the
mother has almost infinite power over the child.
Some perhaps will remember the old Greek story,

Psalm xii. 5; Isa. xiii. 6; xxii. 4; Jer. vi. 7; Joel i. 15; and in
other places.

[1] Heb. שׁדִים.   [2] See Deut. xxxii. 17; and Psalm cvi. 37.

[3] See Parkhurst's *Hebrew Lexicon*, under the words " Shaddai "
and " Sheddim." The " Vale of Siddim," which is mentioned in
Gen. xiv. 3, 10, and which was " well watered as the garden of
the Lord," (Gen. xiii. 10,) seems to have received its name, which
is from the same root, שׁד, from its extreme fertility.

which has come down to us in different forms,[1] of
the babe laid down near some cliff by its mother,
while she was busy with her herd of goats. The
babe, unperceived, crawled to the edge. The mother,
afraid to take a step, lest the child should move
further and fall over the precipice, only uncovered
her breast, and so drew back the infant to her. It
is this figure which God Himself has chosen in this
third name, by which to express to us the nature
of His Almightiness. The Almightiness which will
make His creatures like Him is not of the sword or
of mere force. "Jehovah" bears a sword.[2] But "El
Shaddai," the "Almighty," here revealed to Abram,
is not the "sworded" God. His Almightiness is of
the breast, that is, of bountiful, self-sacrificing, love,
giving and pouring itself out for others. Therefore
He can quiet the restless, as the breast quiets the
child : therefore He can nourish and strengthen, as
the breast nourishes : therefore He can attract, as the
breast attracts, when we are in peril of falling from
Him. This is the "Almighty." And so St. John,
when he receives the vision of One who declares, "I
am Alpha and Omega, the beginning and the ending,
which is, and which was, and which is to come, the
Almighty," marks that He, who says, "I am the
Almighty," is "clothed with a garment down to the
foot, and girt about the paps with a golden girdle."[3]

---

[1] See the *Greek Anthology*, lib. i., cap. 14, § 1.

[2] Deut. xxxii. 41, 42; Ezek. xxi. 3, 5.

[3] Rev. i. 8, 13.—"Girt about the paps." St. John here uses

Here is the woman's dress and the woman's breast, while yet the speaker is "The Almighty." This is "El Shaddai," the "Pourer-forth," who pours Himself out for His creatures; who gives them His life-blood;[1] who "sheds forth His Spirit,"[2] and says, "Come unto me and drink:"[3] "Open thy mouth wide and I will fill it:"[4] and who thus, by the sacrifice of Himself, gives Himself and His very nature to those who will receive Him, that thus His perfect will may be accomplished in them. The blessed Sacrament of the body and blood of Christ is the ceaseless witness of this His giving Himself to us. We may, and we must, "Eat His flesh and drink His blood," if He is to live and work His works in us. Only so, "if we eat His flesh and drink His blood," can we "abide in Him and He in us."[5] Only so, in virtue of His indwelling, can He fulfil His purpose, and be Almighty in us. And yet this giving of Himself involves judgment: self-judgment, if we are obedient: if disobedient, the judgment of the Lord.[6]

This is the truth which the name, "El Shaddai," or "Almighty," everywhere proclaims. But it no-where comes out more clearly than in the record of the LORD's dealings with Abram, when this name,

---

the word μαστὸς, which is the woman's breast or "paps," while μαζὸς is used more indiscriminately for the breast of either man or woman.

[1] Acts xx. 28.	[2] Acts ii. 17, 33.
[3] St. John vii. 37.	[4] Psalm lxxxi. 10.
[5] St. John vi. 53–57.	[6] 1 Cor. xi. 31, 32.

" Almighty," was first revealed to him.   Abram had
long been the heir of promise.   As yet he knew not
" Jehovah," but the LORD had promised to bless him,
and to give him an inheritance, and a seed which
should be as the dust of the earth for multitude.[1]
But Abram was yet childless.   Moved, however, by
the promise of God, in his own energy, and by a
bondmaid, he makes efforts to obtain that which was
to come to him, not in his own strength, but by
God's Almightiness.   Then comes the revelation of
" El Shaddai."   God gives Himself to Abram, and
then Abram perfectly gives himself to God, and by
God is made fruitful.   First, the LORD says, " I am
God Almighty."   Here is the revelation of the
source from which Abram is to receive everything.
Then He adds something to Abram's name.   He
puts something into Abram, which at once changes
him from Abram to Abraham.   What He adds is
the letter *He*, (ה), the chief letter of His own name
" Jehovah,"—that sound which can only be uttered
by an outbreathing,—thus giving to the elect something of His own nature, (for name denotes nature,)
and so by the communication of Himself and of His
outbreath or spirit, moulding His creature to His
own pleasure, that he may be a channel of blessing
to many others.[2]   At once Abram yields himself to

---

[1] Gen. xii. 7 ; and xiii. 15, 16.

[2] May I refer the reader to my *Types of Genesis* (pp. 221,
222,) for a further exposition of the import of this change in
Abram's name.

"God Almighty" in everything:—first, in the outward act of circumcision, that figure of self-judgment and perfect self-surrender, which testified that his hope was not in the flesh, or its energies, but only in the blessed Giver of Himself, by whom alone we can bring forth the fruit that is accepted of Him:—and then no less in the giving up and sacrifice of the much-loved son, who had so long been waited for, and of whom it had been said, "In Isaac shall thy seed be called;" that thus, in the utter renunciation of himself and of his own will, the power of "Almighty God" might be brought in, and the elect in his weakness be made strong, and in his giving up of all be filled with all the fulness of his God.

This was the lesson Abram learnt from the revelation of the name, "El Shaddai." This is the lesson we must all learn, if we too are to know God as "Almighty," able to fulfil His purpose in us, and from fruitless Abrams to make us Abrahams, that is the "fathers of a multitude." [1] From the "Pourer out" of His own Spirit we must receive that Spirit, which will make us give up ourselves in all things; and that Spirit, though freely given, we only receive in the measure that we are emptied of all self-will and self-confidence. Thus are the elect made fruitful. So long as we lack this breath of God, though heirs of promise, we struggle on for our own will, and even in our efforts to gain the promise, as in Abram's dealings with Hagar, are really crossing

[1] See Gen. xvii. 5, *margin.*

Jehovah. When He reveals Himself as the One who gives Himself and His own life to us, and by grace we drink into His Spirit, that "renewing of the Holy Ghost, which He sheds forth abundantly through Jesus Christ our Saviour," [1] then the creature's will is yielded to God, and indeed becomes one with God's will, and therefore God can do what He will, both in us, and with us. Thus God gives Himself to us, just in measure as we give ourselves to Him. Thus His Almightiness comes to us in what appears to be our helplessness. The less of self, the more of God. And the one only thing needed on man's part, to receive all this Almightiness, is the faith to yield oneself to God, and to let Him do what He will with us. Can we so believe as to let God do what He pleases with us? Then as "all things are possible with God," [2] so "all things are possible to him that believeth." [3] "Nations and kings shall come out" of him who is "as good as dead." [4] Nor are the elect alone blessed in all this. Abram is witness, that by this sacrifice of self, through receiving God, blessing comes down on others who are yet far off. All the kindreds of the earth are blessed in the elect, when he can give himself, and his strength, and his life, and all he has to God, that Jehovah's will, so long crossed, may have its way everywhere.

Such is the lesson of the name " El Shaddai,"

---

[1] Tit. iii. 5, 6. [2] St. Mark x. 27.
[3] St. Mark ix. 21. [4] See Gen. xvii. 6; and Heb. xi. 12.

and its connexion with circumcision, that is the self-judgment of the elect, and with the higher fruitfulness which at once results from it.　Its subsequent use in Holy Scripture only illustrates the same great truth, that God by giving Himself and His life to us can make us like Himself, givers of ourselves and of our lives, first to Him, and then by Him to others. The name, " Almighty," occurs forty-eight times in Holy Scripture ; and of these, thirty-one are in the book of Job, and eight in the Revelation; but wherever it occurs, all the allusions to it repeat implicitly or explicitly this same teaching.　I have already referred to the words to Abram, when " El Shaddai " speaks and says, " This is my covenant which ye shall keep. Ye shall circumcise your flesh, and I will make thee exceeding fruitful, and nations and kings shall come out of thee." [1]　But the same thought of fruitfulness is present wherever " El Shaddai " is spoken of.　So when Isaac sends Jacob away to Padan-aram to seek a wife, it is upon " El Shaddai " that he calls, saying, " God Almighty bless thee, and make thee fruitful, and multiply thee, that thou mayest be a multitude of people." [2]　So it is " God Almighty " who says to Jacob, " Be fruitful and multiply : a nation and a company of nations shall be of thee." [3]　It is to " God Almighty " that the same Jacob looks to save his children, when he hears that Simeon is detained in Egypt, and his loved Benjamin is required to go

---

[1] Gen. xvii. 6.　　　　[2] Gen. xxviii. 3.

[3] Gen. xxxv. 11.

there.[1]   And in his blessing upon his sons, it is
under this name, " Almighty," that he blesses Joseph,
with " blessings of the breasts and of the womb." [2]
The name is ever linked with fruit and fruitfulness,
even in cases where it is the loss of fruit that is
lamented.   Thus Naomi twice speaks of her sons'
deaths as " affliction from the Almighty," saying " The
Almighty hath afflicted me." . . . " The Almighty
hath dealt very bitterly with me ; " [3] while, on the
other hand, a " seed that is great, and an offspring as
the grass of the field," is the portion of him who
" despises not the chastening of the Almighty." [4]
For indeed, as with Abram, so with the elect, an
acceptance of the judgment of our flesh is the one
way to receive, and then to minister, the special
blessing which " God Almighty " has prepared for us.

But it is in the book of Job, and in the Revelation,
as I have already said, that we most often find the
name " Almighty," and in both cases for the same
reason.   First as to Job.   One can hardly understand
the continual reference to " El Shaddai " in this book,
without some apprehension of its distinctive lesson.
The aim of the book is to shew the sacrificial use of
God's elect, and how a " perfect and upright " man,
not yet dead to self, by suffering in the flesh is
purged from self, and thus made an instrument,
first to silence Satan, and then, as a priest, appointed
by God, to pray and intercede for those who have

---

[1] Gen. xliii. 14.   [2] Gen. xlix. 25.
[3] Ruth i. 20, 21.   [4] Job v. 17, 25.

condemned him. All know the story, how Job is stripped, first of his wealth and of his sons, and then smitten with a loathsome disease, which is a daily death to him. Three friends come to assist him. "Miserable comforters are they all."[1] They all, in their replies to Job,—Eliphaz more often than the other two,—refer to and dwell upon the name "Almighty."[2] They seem to use it as a sort of proof, that Job's troubles are a judgment for his sins, for "Shaddai" the "Pourer-forth," would (so they argue) surely bless the upright; and if, instead of blessing, He pours out judgments upon Job, then Job must be an evildoer. Eliphaz's one idea of God's government is the exercise of power, especially in punishing the wicked; for when he speaks of the great doings of God, his words are mainly of "crushing," and "destroying," and "causing to perish."[3] Bildad dwells rather on God's justice.[4] Zophar's reproof of Job is based on God's wisdom.[5] But the three friends agree that Job's sorrows must come from sin on his part. None of them have any idea of the sacrificial use of God's elect, or how by the sufferings

---

[1] Job xvi. 2.

[2] Eliphaz uses this name in chap. v. 17; xv. 25; xxii. 3, 17, 23, 25, 26; Bildad, in chap. viii. 3, 5; Zophar in chap. xi. 7. I notice too that while Job's three friends constantly refer to "El," e.g. chap. v. 8; viii. 3, 5, 13, 20; xv. 4, 11, 13, 25; xviii. 21; xx. 15, 29; xxii. 2, 13, 17; xxv. 4, &c., they only twice name "Elohim," and in both these instances they speak of "El" in the same verse. See chap. v. 8; and xx. 29.

[3] Job iv. 19, 20; v. 4; xv. 21.   [4] Job viii. 3, 6, 7, 20.

[5] Job xi. 6–12.

of His saints God may be stilling the enemy and the
avenger. Of these three friends God says, that, with
all their zeal to justify God, "they have not spoken
of me the thing that is right as my servant Job
hath." Eliphaz is singled out for special reproof; [1]
though his view of God's "Almightiness," as being
mere power to "crush" and to "destroy," is still
with many the approved doctrine. Job is accepted
and blessed, spite of all his self-assertion, and his
perplexity, how "God Almighty," being what He is,
can allow him to suffer such varied agonies.[2] But he
understands at last. His pains have wrought his
cure. He needed to be emptied to be better filled ;
and "God Almighty," having emptied, fills His
servant in due time with double blessings.

For the day had been when Job could say, "When
the ear heard me it blessed me : and when the eye
saw me it gave witness to me." [3] The day comes,
when his flesh is judged, and he cries out, "But now
mine eye seeth thee : wherefore I abhor myself, and
repent in dust and ashes." [4] Job, even as we, with all
his uprightness, had to learn how self can live and
please itself, not only in an irreligious and worldly
life, but even in what looks like, and indeed is, real
devotedness. Of this religious self he has to be
stripped. And he is stripped by "El Shaddai." The
judgment of his flesh, which is "the circumcision made

---

[1] Job xlii. 7.

[2] Job xxiv. 1 ; xxi. 2, 35. Thirteen times does Job specially
refer to this name, "Almighty."

[3] Job xxix. 11.   [4] Job xlii. 5, 6.

without hands, in putting off the body of the sins of the flesh," by that death to self, which is indeed " the circumcision of Christ," [1] brings him to the self-emptying and self-despair, where the Lord, as the " Pourer-forth," can fill him out of His Divine fulness. Job at once is freed, and made a blessing. He " prays for his friends, and is accepted," and his " latter end is blessed more than his beginning ; " for he receives " twice as much as he had before, fourteen thousand sheep, and six thousand camels, and a thousand yoke of oxen, and a thousand she asses : he had also seven sons, and three daughters. And after this Job lived a hundred and forty years,"—that is, twice the allotted " three-score and ten,"—" and saw his sons, and his sons' sons, even four generations." [2] Here was fruitfulness indeed. " El Shaddai," whom he had invoked, though He had tried him, had indeed blessed him.

The other book, where the name " Almighty " recurs so often, is that which describes " the Revelation of Jesus Christ, which God gave Him," [3] and which thus opens the course and stages of the manifestation of the Divine life in this outer world, where sin and death are now working. Here the other view of " El Shaddai," as the " Pourer-forth " of judgments, is most prominent ; for the Revelation shews the coming in of God's life, not so much with the elect, (which is seen in Abram, Job, and others,) but rather into the world, which will not willingly

---

[1] Col. ii. 11.   [2] Job xlii. 10–16.   [3] Rev. i. 1.

receive it, or which, if in some sense it is accepted, only perverts it. And the result is, that as the pourings forth of the breast, not properly received, may choke the babe:—as the rain from heaven, not drunk in by the earth, may cause a torrent, which for the time brings only desolation:—as drinking Christ's cup may be a drinking of judgment or damnation:[1] —so the pouring out of the Divine life and Spirit into the world may, and indeed must, bring judgment, that so through judgment, if in no other way, the true Kingdom may be brought in. The elect who willingly receive the Word and outbreath of " El Shaddai," shew that even an obedient reception involves the judgment of the flesh. How much sorer must this judgment be to the world which will not receive God! If the Word or Spirit comes to such, it must be in double judgment. It is judgment to the willing elect: how much more to those who will not open their hearts to welcome it! For " all flesh is grass, and the goodliness thereof is as the flower of the field. The grass withereth, the flower fadeth: because the Spirit of the Lord bloweth upon it."[2] Therefore in the Revelation of Jesus Christ, which God gives Him in the world, we read so often of the " Almighty," and of the outpourings of " El Shaddai," as causing judgments. His most precious gifts bring chastening and judgment to His rebellious creatures. Yet spite of the judgment, nay rather by it, the Kingdom comes.

---

[1] 1 Cor. xi. 29.　　　　　[2] Isa. xl. 6, 7.

In the Revelation we are shewn the successive stages of its coming. And it is especially at the end, when the best gifts are given, that there is the sorest judgment. Three stages of the coming of the Lord are revealed, under the figures of the Opening of the Sealed Book or Word,[1] the Sounding forth of Trumpets, and the Pouring forth of Golden Vials. Connected with all these is the name " Almighty : " once in connexion with the Loosing of the Seals:[2] once with the Trumpets :[3] and four times in connexion with the Pouring out of the Vials, and the final coming of the Lord.[4] The Lamb first comes as the Looser of the Seals. He who had been the Pourer out of His own blood from the beginning, for He is " the Lamb slain from the foundation of the world,"[5] begins by giving forth His Word in opening the Seals, that is the mystery of God.[6] These are judgments to the world.[7] But there is still sorer judgment when the Breath of God goes forth through the Trumpets, and smites a " third part " of the earth, and the sea, and rivers, and sun, and all things of this world.[8] Lastly

---

[1] " Book " or " Word " are the same in Hebrew, דבר ; see Gen. xv. 1, 4 ; xxiv. 30, 52 ; 1 Chron. xxix. 29 ; 2 Chron. ix. 29 ; xii. 5, &c. A book is a word.

[2] Rev. iv. 8.   [3] Rev. xi. 17.

[4] Rev. xv. 5 ; xvi. 7, 14 ; xix. 15 ; Isaiah and Joel also both foresee, that " the day of the Lord shall come as a destruction from the Almighty." Isa. xiii. 6 ; and Joel i. 15.

[5] Rev. v. 9 ; and xiii. 8.

[6] Rom. xvi. 25, 26 ; and Eph. iii. 4, 5.   [7] Rev. vi. 1-17.

[8] Rev. viii. 2, to ix. 21. Compare this " third part " with what St. Paul says of man's nature, " spirit, soul, and body," in 1 Thess. v. 23.

we have the final pouring out of the Golden Vials of the true temple, which smites, not a " third part " only, but the whole creature or creation. In these is filled up the wrath of God.[1]

And yet, as William Law said long ago, " the Love that brought forth the existence of all things changes not through the fall of its creatures, but is continually at work to bring back all fallen nature and creatures. All that passes for a time between God and His fallen creature is but one and the same thing, working for one and the same end ; and though this is called ' wrath,' and that called ' punishment,' ' curse,' and ' death,' it is all from the beginning to the end nothing but the work of the first creating Love, and means nothing else, and does nothing else, but those works of purifying fire, which must and alone can burn away all that dark evil, which separates the creature from its first-created union with God. God's providence, from the fall to the restitution of all things, is doing the same thing as when He said to the dark chaos of fallen nature, ' Let there be light.' He still says, and will continue saying, the same thing, till there is no evil of darkness left in nature and creature. God creating, God illuminating, God sanctifying, God threatening and punishing, God forgiving and redeeming, are all but one and the same essential, immutable, never-ceasing working of the Divine Nature. That in God, which illuminates and glorifies saints and angels in

[1] Rev. xv. 1; and xvi. 1–24.

heaven, is that same working of the Divine Nature, which wounds, pains, punishes, and purifies, sinners upon earth. And every number of destroyed sinners, whether thrown by Noah's flood or Sodom's brimstone into the terrible furnace of a life insensible of anything but new forms of misery until the judgment day, must through the all-working, all-redeeming love of God, which never ceases, come at last to know that they had lost and have found again such a God of love as this." [1] The end is a " new creation," where " there shall be no more death, nor sorrow, nor pain ; " [2] where " the Lord God Almighty and the Lamb shall be the glory and the light " for ever. [3]

Such is " El Shaddai," " God Almighty," who works His will in His elect by giving Himself to them, that they may give themselves to Him, and then by Him be blessed to others, in and by that circumcision or self-judgment, which makes them vessels, through which He can minister His own fulness. In a word, like Christ, they are made sacramental,—pledges of what God can do in man, and means by which others may receive the same blessing. God, by the sacrifice of Himself, has made them partakers of His nature. They, as His sons and daughters, make others partakers of the same nature. Their separation to Him fits them for their work ; as He says, " Come out, and be separate, and touch not the unclean thing, and

---

[1] Law's *Address to the Clergy,* pp. 171, 172.

[2] Rev. xxi. 4, 5.   [3] Rev. xxi. 22–24.

ye shall be my sons and daughters, saith the Lord
Almighty."[1] Thus they also become " breasted " and
"pourers forth." In them is fulfilled the promise to
Jerusalem, that " those who love her may suck and
be satisfied with the breasts of her consolations ; that
they may milk out and be delighted with the abun-
dance of her glory."[2] Out of their belly flow rivers
of living water.[3] By faith they minister the Spirit
and work miracles.[4]

If all this is seen we may better understand why
the Church makes such use of this name, " Almighty,"
and begins so many of her prayers with the words,
" Almighty and most merciful Father," or " Almighty
God."[5] For by this name she claims His Spirit,
confessing that He gives all, while by the same name
she reminds her children, how, in His very gifts,
those who eat and drink unworthily may eat and
drink their own judgment. As we call upon this
name let us remember all its rich and solemn import, and by grace be made, not only, like old
Adam, " living souls," but, like Christ our Lord,
" quickening spirits " also to all around us.[6]

Shall we not bless God for this name revealed
to men of faith ? Shall we not " abide under the
shadow of the Almighty " ?

---

[1] 2 Cor. vi. 17, 18 ; the only place in the New Testament
where the name " Almighty " occurs, except in the Apocalypse.

[2] Isa. lxvi. 10, 11.   [3] St. John vii. 38.

[4] Gal. iii. 5.

[5] See the Prayer Book generally, and specially the Communion
Service.   [6] 1 Cor. xv. 45.

4

MOST HIGH GOD, OR EL ELYON

WE have seen how the view of God, revealed to
Abram under the name " El Shaddai," or " Almighty,"
reconciles, so far as the elect are concerned, the apparent contradiction suggested by the first two names
of God, and by the varying aspects of His nature
which are brought before us in them. The name,
" Most High," which we are now to consider, throws
yet further light on the same point, revealing God in
relation to those who are not Abram's seed, who
nevertheless possess a priesthood of an order which
is earlier and greater than that of the elect, and yet
not in opposition to it. This name, " Most High
God," is revealed in connexion with Melchisedek, the
King of Salem, in the days of Abram. Melchisedek,
we are told, was " priest of the Most High God ; "
and it was through him that Abram also received
the knowledge of this name ; for it was only after
Abram's meeting with Melchisedek that he says, " I
have lifted up my hand unto the LORD, the Most
High God, possessor of heaven and earth." [1] The
elect's knowledge of this name therefore is somehow
connected with his knowledge of Melchisedek, and of

[1] Gen. xiv. 22.

the special nature of his priesthood, as " priest of the
Most High."

Now that there is something very deep and special
in the knowledge of this name, and of this priesthood, is obvious from the way in which the writer of
the Epistle to the Hebrews introduces what he has to
say respecting it.   The passage is in the fifth, sixth,
and seventh, chapters of that Epistle.   There we
see that the writer, having in the earlier portion of
his Epistle spoken, first, of "God," who "has built
all things," and who "made them by His Son,"[1]
whose "word is quick and powerful," for He is "appointed Heir of all things;"[2] and then, secondly, of
the "Lord," who "remains the same, and whose
years shall not fail,"[3] who "is and shall be what He
is," to whose words therefore "we ought to give the
more earnest heed, lest at any time we let them
slip;"[4] and then, thirdly, of One who gives His
Spirit to men, so that the elect are partakers of His
life, as he says, "He that sanctifieth, and they which
are sanctified are all of one,"[5] which is the truth
taught under the title, "The Almighty," who in the
power of His outbreathing makes His elect partakers
of His nature;—the writer, having thus referred to
the three names of God which we have already considered, namely, "God," "Lord," and "Almighty,"
says that he wishes, "if God permit," to go on to
speak of One, who, being a "Priest after the order

---

[1] Heb. i. 2; and iii. 4.   [2] Heb. iv. 12.
[3] Heb. i. 12.   [4] Heb. ii. 1.   [5] Heb. ii. 11.

of Melchisedek," is " Priest of the Most High God ; " [1]
" of whom," he adds, " we have many things to say,
and hard to be uttered, seeing that ye are dull of
hearing ; for when for the time ye ought to be
teachers, ye have need that one teach you again
which be the first principles of the oracles of God ;
and are become such as have need of milk, and not
of strong meat." But at this point the writer suddenly breaks off, and makes a long digression, which
occupies the latter part of the fifth, and the whole
of the sixth, chapter of his Epistle.

What he says in this digression is in substance
this :—" You ought, considering the time you have
been believers, to be able to go on from the first
principles of the doctrine of Christ, which are as
milk for babes, to the deeper truths of revelation,
which are the meat for men of full age." The " first
principles " consist of three things : first, " repentance from dead works ; " secondly, " faith towards
God ; " and thirdly, a certain " doctrine " or teaching,
as to " baptisms, and the laying on of hands, and the
resurrection of the dead, and eternal judgment."
Of these the first, touching " repentance," is connected with " Jehovah," the just and holy LORD : the
second, namely " faith towards God," takes us back
to " Elohim's " changeless love in virtue of relationship : while the third, containing a fourfold doctrine,
—as to " baptisms," which are purifications ; as to
" laying on of hands," which are gifts bestowed ; and

[1] Heb. v. 6, 10; and vii. 1.

as to " resurrection " and " eternal judgment," which are the varying results of the working of God's Spirit on the creature, whether obedient or disobedient,—is all directly connected with the knowledge of " El Shaddai," the " Pourer-forth " of His own life, to make His creatures fruitful. These truths, which comprise all that the majority of Christians now consider essential, are by the Apostle here all spoken of as simply " first principles." " Leaving these," he says, " let us go on unto perfection." " And this," he adds, " we will do, if God permit." But God may not permit. For there is a peculiar peril in the carnal reception of the higher truth, which is contained in the name " Most High," and in the doctrine of the " priesthood of Melchisedek," which is connected with this revelation. " For," as the Apostle goes on to say, " it is impossible for those who were once enlightened, and have tasted of the heavenly gift, and been made partakers of the Holy Ghost, and have tasted the good word of God, and the powers of the world to come, if they shall fall away, to renew them again to repentance ; seeing they crucify to themselves the Son of God afresh, and put Him to an open shame ; " for this knowledge may be like the rain, which not only makes the ground bring forth herbs meet for them by whom it is dressed, but may also stimulate it to produce an increased growth of thorns and briars ; so that by this higher knowledge a man may be even worse than he was before, " nigh unto cursing, whose end is to be burned." There is therefore a special peril, as well as blessing, in the knowledge of this name, " Most High." An awful pride may be the result of an unsanctified reception of it. If our self-will is chastened by it, we may be made more perfect and enlightened; but if our will is only stimulated to greater self-confidence and self-assertion by the deeper truth received, a more awful judgment can only result from such knowledge. As old John Bunyan said, when asked, what doctrine was the worst,—" I know of none so dangerous as the truth of God received carnally." The knowledge of the " Most High " is therefore " a secret." [1] A Divine warning mercifully meets us on our approach to it.

With this warning, which is that of the Apostle, when he would speak of the " priest of the Most High," I proceed to say what little I may respecting this name of God, and the circumstances under which it is revealed in Holy Scripture. Both the name itself, and its special connexion with things and persons outside the election, if we can read their import, are full of significance.

First, as to the name itself, " Most High God : " in Hebrew, " El Elyon : " [2] the " El " here is the same as in the name " El Shaddai," and, here as there, expresses the same idea of God as " Might " or " Power." [3] What is further revealed here is that this " God," or " El," is the " Most High," and as

---

[1] Psalm xci. 1.   [2] Heb. אל עליון.
[3] See above, pp. 64, 65.

such "Possessor of heaven and earth." [1]   Now this
name "Elyon," or "Most High," like some others
which are used of God, is at times applied in Holy
Scripture to things and persons of this world; but,
wherever it is so used, its special and distinctive
sense is always, that the person or thing it speaks of
is the highest of a series or order of like natures.   It
is used of the "highest basket" of a tier of baskets :[2]
of the "nation high above all nations ; " [3] of the " king
higher than other kings; " [4] of " chambers higher
than other chambers." [5]   A different word is used
when it is said that the " heavens are higher than
the earth ; " [6] or that the " clouds are higher than a
man." [7]   Thus the word, " Elyon," or " Most High,"
here applied to God, reveals, that, though He is the
" Highest," there are others below Him, endowed
by Him with like natures, and therefore in some
way related to Him ; but that, because He is the
" Highest," He has power to rule and turn them as
He will, should they be disobedient or seek to exalt
themselves against Him.   For " the Most High

---

[1] Gen. xiv. 19, 22.   [2] Gen. xl. 17.

[3] Deut. xxvi. 19.   [4] Psalm lxxxix. 27.

[5] Ezek. xli. 7 ; and xlii. 5.   For other illustrations of this,
compare, the "upper watercourse," 2 Chron. xxxii. 30 ; the "upper
pool," 2 Kings xviii. 17 ; Isa. vii. 3 ; and xxxvi. 2 ; the "upper
gate," 2 Kings xv. 35 ; 2 Chron. xxiii. 20 ; the "upper court," Jer.
xxxvi. 10 ; and the "high house," Neh. iii. 25 ; in all which places
the word "Elyon" is used, to describe the "pool," or "gate," or
"court," or "house," higher than other "pools," or "gates," or
"courts," or "houses."

[6] Isa. lv. 9.   [7] Job xxxv. 5.

doeth according to His will, in the armies of heaven, and among the inhabitants of the earth ; and none can stay His hand, or say unto Him, What doest thou ? His dominion is an everlasting dominion, and His kingdom is from generation to generation." [1]

Who then are those below Him, who are endowed with like natures ? First, angels are " sons of God : " [2] even fallen angels, whatever the depth of their fall, are partakers of a nature which is descended from Him.[3] This it is which makes their fall so awful. These are the powers of heaven,[4] which exalted themselves, figured by the kings of Tyre and Babylon of old, whose " heart was lifted up because of their beauty, and who corrupted their wisdom by reason of their brightness ; " who " said, I am El : I sit in the seat of God : " " I will exalt my throne above the stars of El : I will ascend above the heights of the clouds : I will be like the Most High." [5] But there are others, who " for a little while are lower than the angels," [6] who are also " children of the Most High." This is the point constantly referred to in the Psalms which speak of the " Most High," especially in the Psalm which our Lord quotes, where men are called " gods : "—" Is it not written in your law, I said, Ye are gods, and all of you the children of the Most High ?" [7] For man was " created in the

---

[1] Dan. iv. 34, 35.

[2] Job xxxviii. 7 ; Psalm xxix. 1 ; and lxxxix. 6.

[3] Job i. 6 ; and ii. 1.   [4] Eph. vi. 12.

[5] See Ezek. xxviii. 2–17 ; and Isa. xiv. 12, 13.

[6] Heb. ii. 7.   [7] Psalm lxxxii. 1, 6 ; and St. John x. 34.

image of God." [1]   He may not know it, for he is
fallen, and become " even as a beast ; " [2] for awhile
without his true inheritance ; yet is he in his fall a
fallen son ; for " Adam was son of God," [3] and " the
gifts and calling of God are without repentance." [4]
Therefore even to unconverted Gentiles, bowing to
idols, Paul could quote as truth their poet's words,
" For we also are His offspring," [5] and say again to
carnal Corinthians, that " the head of every man is
Christ," and that " man is the image and glory of
God," [6] like the " lost silver," [7] bearing something of
the image of his Maker, dimmed and defaced as that
image may be through sin.   Certainly when one
thinks what man can do, even in his fall, and in this
life, which is " but as a vapour, which appeareth for
a little while, and then vanisheth away," [8] how he
can weigh the earth, measure the stars, calculate to
a moment when some planet in its rapid course shall
pass between us and the sun, and tell where on one
part of the surface of this moving globe this shall be
seen, while on other parts of the same globe it shall
be invisible : how he can make the lightning carry
his words, under the sea or over the earth : how he
makes the sunlight give us pictures of every seen
creature : nay more, how he can speak the words of

---

[1] Gen. i. 27. I have already referred to the connexion between ברא, *to create*, and בֵּן, *a son*.

[2] Psalm xl. 12, 20 ; and lxxiii. 22.

[3] St. Luke iii. 38.

[4] Rom. xi. 29.

[5] Acts xvii. 28.

[6] 1 Cor. xi. 3, 7.

[7] St. Luke xv. 8.

[8] St. James iv. 14.

God Himself, for God speaks both through him and
to him :—when but for a moment one considers this,
what does it all witness, but that man is even here a
son of the " Most High,"—a fallen son, even a dead
son, leprous, palsied, mad, or blind, not knowing his
Father,—nevertheless a son ; and because a son, never
to be forsaken by Him from whom he came; for " the
fathers must lay up for the children, and not the
children for the fathers." [1]   There is surely peril in
this high truth, yet there is rich blessing also ; for
the " Most High " cannot deny Himself, and therefore, even if we forget our relationship to Him, can
and surely will overthrow and overturn and overcome
us, till He has again His due place in us for our
blessing.   For He is " over all," [2] the " God of
gods," [3] the " King of kings and Lord of lords," [4]
" of whom, and through whom, and to whom are all
things." [5]

This is the truth first revealed in Scripture
through Melchisedek, who was " king of Salem, and
priest of the Most High."   Apparently of Canaan's
race,[6] for he dwelt among them as one of their

---

[1] 2 Cor. xii. 14.   [2] Rom. ix. 5.   [3] Psalm cxxxvi. 2.
[4] Rev. xix. 16.   [5] Rom. xi. 36.
[6] This was the view of some of the most learned of the
Fathers, Hippolytus, Eusebius, Theodoret, and others, (see Jerome,
in his Epist. lxxviii, on this subject,) and seems also to have been
the opinion of Josephus. (*Antiqq.* i. 10. § 2.)   The name of the
king of Jerusalem in the days of Joshua, Adonizedek, supports
this view ; Adonizedek being substantially the same as Melchisedek, the one meaning " lord," the other " king," of righteousness.

kings, he does not seem to have known,—certainly
he does not speak of,—" Elohim," the covenant-
keeping God, or of " Jehovah," the righteous LORD,
who yet suffers with His fallen creatures, or of " El
Shaddai," the Breasted God, who gives His own
Spirit to His people. All these are names which are
the special portion of the elect. But he knew
" Elyon," the " Most High," whose name preserved,
even among the Gentiles, the truth, however much
abused, that in God's creation there are " thrones
and dominions and principalities and powers," called
" gods," [1] which are more or less akin to God;
and that though for a season lower than these,
and under a curse for sin, men also are " children
of the Most High," and as such predestined to an
inheritance which must be one of rich blessing.
Strange and yet most certain, that this truth, so
dimly seen by Israel, should have been kept by the
Gentile world. Yet so it was. The old mythologies
are full of stories of men who were sons of gods,
these gods being sons of a higher God, who was the
Lord of all. Melchisedek shews how even a son of
Canaan kept up the same tradition of man's high
nature; while what is recorded of his people reveals,
how in this faith, often to their own hurt, they
sought, by " witches, and consulters with familiar
spirits, and wizards, and necromancers," [2] to hold
converse with the unseen powers, which they recog-

[1] Col. i. 16; and Psalm xcvii. 7.
[2] Deut. xviii. 10-12.

nised as above, and yet not wholly severed from, them. Their idea of God was terribly perverted, but it was the perversion of a great truth, that God had sons, and that man was one; a truth which the elect nation, through their bondage in Egypt, had lost perhaps even more than far-off Gentiles. The name, " El Elyon," preserved this truth of God's relation to "thrones and dominions" far below Him, and that even men, under a curse, and fallen from Him, are indeed " His offspring."

All this, and secrets of grace, even more profound, are revealed yet hidden in what is recorded of Melchisedek. For the fact that man is son of God involved a further relationship. Man as son of God must be a priest; for as God, because He is love, cannot but sacrifice, so man, the son of God, and inheriting His nature, must also sacrifice. The name, " El Shaddai," revealed much. It told how God is specially related to the elect, and that through circumcision, that is the judgment of the flesh, a new life shall be brought forth, a life, like Isaac's, of sacrifice, and yet of rest, in and through whom all nations shall be blessed. The name " El Elyon " reveals more,—namely, that Gentiles, like Canaan, though doomed to judgment here, have, in their relation to the " Most High," the pledge of sure and high blessing, even to be priests in virtue of their sonship. This truth shadowed in Melchisedek, who is brought before us in Scripture, as " without genealogy or descent, having neither beginning of

days, nor end of life, but made like unto the Son of
God,"[1] is the blessed truth which is perfectly revealed
in Christ, the Son of God, who, because He is One
to whom God says, " Thou art my son, to day have I
begotten thee," is " priest after the order of Melchisedek." [2]   Christ is the witness of man's true
nature—that he is son of God.   He serves as
priest, because he is a son of God.   His priesthood, as the Apostle says, is " not after the law of a
carnal commandment, but after the power of an
endless life." [3]   The priesthood after the order of
Aaron is a priesthood based on a commandment; [4]
that commandment being required by man's fall, and
the consequent separation between God and man,
and man and man.   But the priesthood of man, as
man, that is, as son of God, for " Adam was son of
God," [5] is based on the participation of the Divine
nature.   And though that nature is spoilt and perverted by the fall, and man, in ignorance of God
through the serpent's lie, regarding Him as an
Exactor rather than a Giver, ceases himself to be a
giver or offerer of himself in willing sacrifice ; yet
is his nature in its source and essence still Divine.
Even in its fall it is the fall of something heavenly.
The priesthood of one so related to God must be in
virtue of a life, not of a commandment, and as such
far greater than any priesthood or righteousness of
law.   The " priest of the Most High " preserves this

---

[1] Heb. vii. 3.   [2] Heb. v. 5, 6.   [3] Heb. vii. 16.
[4] Heb. vii. 5.   [5] St. Luke iii. 38.

truth, and is the means of teaching it even to him
who had received the promises.

Now a priest in virtue of sonship, inheriting God's
nature, will necessarily inherit all the varied virtues
of that nature. The Apostle calls our attention to
this fact in pointing out that the "priest of the Most
High" is "King of righteousness" and "King of
peace."[1] In this double title we see again the union
of the two great truths revealed apart in "Jehovah"
and "Elohim." For "Jehovah" is righteous: and the
"priest of the Most High" is "king of righteousness."
Elohim's covenant and oath pledge unbroken union
and peace: and the "priest of the Most High"
is also "king of peace." Thus he is witness that
"righteousness and peace shall kiss each other,"[2]
through the power which is in the "Most High" to
reconcile all antagonisms. It is hard to utter even
a little of the wonders which are figured here.
Melchisedek, though a Gentile, and of Canaan's
cursed seed, "blesses Abram," who has already
received the promise, that the land of Canaan shall
be his for ever;—a promise only to be fulfilled by
the casting out of Canaan and his seed;—and further
"blesses the Most High God, who has delivered
Abram's enemies into his hands;" while Abram, the
heir of promise, "pays tithes," as a debtor to one,
whose people are to be judged and cast out for the
fulfilment of the promises.[3] To crown all, Canaan,

---

[1] Heb. vii. 2.   [2] Psalm lxxxv. 10.
[3] Gen. xiv. 19, 20.

the land of the cursed, for "Cursed is Canaan,"[1] becomes the land of promise, and the inheritance of the elect.[2] But Christ has opened all the secret. Man as man is son of God. He may be, and is, for awhile like Canaan under a curse; but even so, because his God is the "Most High," he is also the heir of boundless blessing. With such a God the very curse became a blessing; judgment is mercy; and death the way of life. The cursed are to be blessed, and blessed through the elect, who are but "a kind of firstfruits of God's creatures;"[3] while the elect, who have accepted the judgment of their flesh, in circumcision, are appointed to judge those who cannot judge themselves, for "the saints shall judge the world;"[4] that so "the creature may be delivered from the bondage of corruption, into the glorious liberty of the children of God."[5] Therefore those who must be judged, like Canaan and his seed, bless both the elect, who shall judge them, and the "Most High," who gives His elect victory over the foe which has led their brethren captive.[6] The true "Priest after the order of Melchisedek," the Son of Man and Son of God, has set this in a light never to be dimmed, though few as yet see all its significance. As in the flesh, and linked with all, He was accursed, and yet is blessed:[7] condemned in the flesh, yet justified in

[1] Gen. ix. 25. [2] Psalm cv. 11.

[3] Rom. xi. 16; St. James i. 18; Rev. xiv. i. 4.

[4] 1 Cor. vi. 2. [5] Rom. viii. 21.

[6] Gen. xiv. 17, 18; and Heb. vii. 1.

[7] Gal. iii. 13; Rev. v. 12.

the Spirit.[1] As the elect, He will judge the world;
and His judgment, when with the sword, which goeth
out of His mouth, He will smite all flesh, both of free
and bond, will save the world.[2] He Himself is the
witness how the judged through judgment shall be
blessed, and how the Judge only judges to bring in
righteousness and peace.

And the further title, which is added when
the name "Most High" is first revealed, namely
"Possessor of heaven and earth,"[3] throws yet clearer
light on the view of God here opened to us. For the
word translated "Possessor,"[4] comes directly from
a verb, which, though in our Authorised Version
variously rendered to "buy," or "purchase," or "possess,"[5] means primarily to "*contain*" or "*hold*."[6] It
therefore describes One "in whom we live, and move,
and have our being;"[7] "in whom all things consist;"[8]
"for whom are all things, and by whom are all
things."[9] The "Most High" is "Possessor" of all,
"of heaven and earth," of church and world: and this
His rightful claim He never foregoes, though angels

---

[1] 1 Tim. iii. 16; 1 Pet. iii. 18.

[2] Rev. xix. 15, 18; and Psalm lxxii. 8.

[3] Gen. xiv. 19.   [4] Heb. קנה.

[5] See Gen. xxv. 10; xxxiii. 19; xxxix. 1; xlvii. 19, 20, 22;
Exod. xv. 10; xxi. 2; Lev. xxii. 11; Deut. xxxii. 6; Neh. v. 8;
Psalm lxxiv. 2; lxxviii. 54; and in many other places.

[6] So Parkhurst: see *Heb. Lex.* in loc. This primary sense of
this word, as meaning to "*contain*," or "*hold*," explains its use
in Gen. iv. 1; Prov. i. 5; iv. 5, 7; xvi. 16, and in other places,
where it is translated "*get*" or "*attain*."

[7] Acts xvii. 28.   [8] Col. i. 17   [9] Heb. ii. 10.

or men for awhile may act as self-proprietors. Thus this name answers the question of the Apostle, "Is He the God of the Jews only? Is He not also of the Gentiles? Yes, of the Gentiles also."[1] For He is "the God of the spirits of all."[2] He has said, "All souls are mine."[3] "All lands" should "know," that "it is He that hath made us, and not we ourselves: we are His people, and the sheep of His pasture."[4] And the true elect, like Abram, though through long years they may not have seen this,—for the elect are slow to receive things outside their own election,—when it is shewn them by the "Priest of the Most High," at once accept the blessed truth, saying, "I have lifted up my hand to the Most High, Possessor of heaven and earth."[5] Thus does Abram learn from a Gentile what the chief Apostle learnt later through the centurion of the Italian band, that the elect "should call no man common or unclean;"[6] "for the same Lord over all is rich unto all that call upon Him; for whosoever shall call upon the name of the Lord shall be saved."[7]

Such is the first mention of the "Most High" in Holy Scripture; but in every passage where the name occurs, its special import is the same, revealing the relationship of God to all, even to the world outside the election, and that, where men either cannot or will not judge themselves, the "Most High" even through judgment will carry out in them His own

---

[1] Rom. iii. 29.   [2] Numb. xvi. 22.   [3] Ezek. xviii. 4.
[4] Psalm c. 1, 3.   [5] Gen. xiv. 22.
[6] Acts x. 28.   [7] Rom. x. 12.

purpose. Every reference to the name repeats this teaching. In the books of Moses we find it only in three places,—first in the words we have considered, in connexion with Melchisedek, then in Balaam's prophecy, and lastly in the song of Moses,—but in each case this name is either in the mouth of a Gentile, or in reference to the Gentile world, and God's relation to it. Balaam, who " came from Aram, out of the mountains of the east," [1] says, that he " had heard the words of El, and knew the knowledge of the Most High, and saw the vision of the Almighty." What does he see but the judgment of the nations, of " Sheth, and Moab, and Amalek, and Asshur," while " out of Jacob shall come He that shall have dominion " ? [2] The words of the song of Moses no less distinctly link the nations with the " Most High : " — " When the Most High divided the nations their inheritance, when He separated the sons of Adam, He set the bounds of the peoples according to the number of the children of Israel ; " thus caring for Gentiles, though at the same time witnessing that " Jehovah's portion is His people," and that He has chosen Jacob for a special purpose and for special blessings.[3] In the Historic Books, from Joshua to Esther, the name " Most High " never occurs, except in a Psalm of David's, which is inserted in the history ; [4] but the omission is characteristic, for these books are the record of the elect, and of their relation to " Jehovah,"

---

[1] Numb. xxiii. 7.
[2] Numb. xxiv. 16.
[3] Deut. xxxii. 8, 9.
[4] 2 Sam. xxii. 14.

and the name "Most High" rather belongs to the world outside the election. In the Psalms the name is oftener referred to; but, wherever it is used, we find, if not a direct mention of the Gentile world, and its final subjection to the "Most High," yet a recognition of its claims and of God's universal providence. Thus in the eighty-third Psalm, where we read of the "enemies of God," "Edom, Moab, and the Hagarenes, the Philistines with the inhabitants of Tyre, and Asshur," the end is foreseen, that "they shall be confounded, and put to shame, and perish; that they may seek thy name, and know that thou, whose name alone is Jehovah, art the Most High over all the earth."[1] It is the same in the eighty-seventh Psalm, where, foreseeing that "of Zion it shall be said, The Highest (or "Most High") Himself shall establish her," "mention" is no less made of "Rahab, and Babylon, and of Philistia, and Tyre, with Ethiopia," that "this man was born there."[2] To the same effect, in the Psalm already referred to, from which our Lord quotes the words, "I said, Ye are gods, and all of you the children of the Most High," the conclusion is, "Arise, O God, and judge the earth, for thou shalt inherit all nations."[3] Thus again in the Psalm, which speaks perhaps more clearly than any other of God's kingdom over all nations, the Psalmist's reason why all should praise Him is, that "the Lord, Most High, is terrible: He

---

[1] Psalm lxxxiii. 6, 7, 16, 17, 18.

[2] Psalm lxxxvii. 4, 5.   [3] Psalm lxxxii. 6, 8.

is a great King over all the earth. He shall subdue
the peoples under us, and the nations under our feet;
for God is the King over all the earth ; and the princes
of the peoples are gathered together to be[1] the
people of the God of Abraham ; for the shields of
the earth belong unto God.   He is greatly exalted."[2]

And I notice that the elect themselves, when,
either for their own or for Israel's sin, they are cast
out, almost as Gentiles, "far from God's holy hill and
from His tabernacle," seem instinctively to turn to
this name " Most High," as a ground of hope, whatever
may be their trouble or unworthiness.   Thus David,
"when the Philistines took him in Gath," cries to the
" Most High."[3]   Again, " when he fled from Saul
in the cave," his words are, " I will cry unto God,
Most High ; unto God that performeth all things for
me."[4]   Again, when fleeing from his son Absalom,
he hears "the words of Cush, the Benjamite," he
accepts the Gentiles' place, invoking the " Most
High."[5]   For under this name all may find hope.
It is the witness for ever, that, whatever our condition,
there yet is help for us in Him from whom we came.

But there is perhaps no better illustration of the
import of this name than the way it is used in the
case of Nebuchadnezzar, who is set before us in the
book of Daniel as the great head of Gentile power.

---

[1] So the Revised Version.
[2] Psalm xlvii. 1–9.
[3] Psalm lvi. 2, and title.
[4] Psalm lvii. 2, and title.
[5] Psalm vii. 17, and title.   Compare also Psalm ix. 2, 5 ;
xviii. 13 ; and xxi. 7.

In him we find the Adamic dominion almost repeated :
—" Thou, O king, art a king of kings, for the God of
heaven hath given thee a kingdom, and wheresoever
the children of men dwell, the beasts of the field, and
the fowls of heaven, hath He given into thine hand,
and hath made thee ruler over all." [1]　But his heart
is lifted up : through self-exaltation he loses his
understanding, till by judgment he is brought to
know the " Most High." What is written of him
requires no comment. " The king spake, and said,
Is not this great Babylon, that I have built, by the
might of my power, and for the honour of my
majesty ? While the word was in the king's mouth,
there fell a voice from heaven, saying, O king
Nebuchadnezzar, to thee it is spoken ; The kingdom
is departed from thee. And they shall drive thee
from men, and thy dwelling shall be with the beasts,
and seven times shall pass over thee, until thou know
that the Most High ruleth in the kingdom of men,
and giveth it to whomsoever He will. The same
hour was Nebuchadnezzar driven from men, and did
eat grass as oxen, till his hairs were grown like
eagles' feathers, and his nails like birds' claws. And
at the end of the days I Nebuchadnezzar lifted up
mine eyes to heaven, and mine understanding re-
turned unto me, and I blessed the Most High, whose
dominion is an everlasting dominion, and His kingdom from generation to generation." [2]　Are there not

[1] Dan. ii. 37, 38.

[2] Dan. iv. 30-34. See too Dan. v. 18-22, where the same

yet such souls, some of the grandest of the sons of
men, who know neither " Elohim," nor " El Shaddai,"
nor " Jehovah," but who like Nebuchadnezzar shall
be brought to know that the " Most High " ruleth,
and through His rule shall regain their understanding ? This, if I err not, is the " secret of the Most
High." [1] Souls outside the election shall own His
power ; and the saints,—here, in their relation to the
world, called the " saints of the Most High,"—shall
have judgment given to them, and shall " possess the
kingdom." [2]

I will only add that the indirect allusions to the
worship of the " Most High," wherever we find such
in Holy Scripture, always shew something wider and
simpler than that which was divinely ordained for
the elect people. To recur to the first place in
which the name occurs. Melchisedek, "priest of the
Most High," is presented to us, not only "without
genealogy," [3] as the Apostle says, but also without
a temple, and without blood, offering simply " bread
and wine," when He blesses the " Most High," and at
the same time pronounces upon Abram the blessing
of the " Most High." [4] For " the Most High dwelleth
not in temples made with hands ; " [5] " neither is He
worshipped as though He needed anything, seeing
He giveth to all life, and breath, and all things." [6]

name, " Most High," is used by Daniel when he interprets to
Belshazzar the " writing on the wall."

[1] Psalm xci. 1.	[2] Dan. vii. 18, 22, 25, 27.
[3] Heb. vii. 3.	[4] Gen. xiv. 18, 20.
[5] Acts vii. 48.	[6] Acts xvii. 25, 26.

Therefore in the Psalm which says, " The Mighty
God hath spoken, and called the earth from the
rising of the sun unto the going down thereof," His
question, to those who would satisfy Him with
" bullocks out of their house, and he-goats out of
their folds," is, " Will I eat the flesh of bulls, or
drink the blood of goats ? Offer unto God thanks-
giving, and pay thy vows unto the Most High ; and
call upon me in the day of trouble : I will deliver
thee, and thou shalt glorify me." [1] What the
" Most High " delights in is a life in accordance with
His own. This is the witness of His beloved Son, in
the Gospel which links Him with all men, and in
which alone of the Gospels the title " Most High " is
to be found,[2] where He says, " Love your enemies,
and do good and lend, hoping for nothing again ;
and ye shall be children of the Most High, for He is
kind unto the unthankful and to the evil." [3] " In every
nation he that feareth Him, and worketh righteousness, is accepted with Him." [4]

Such is the teaching of the name " Most High."
In it more than in any other name, we have the revelation of God's relationship to man as man, and of
the unchangeableness of that relationship, spite of
the change which sin has wrought in man's condition. Need I say again that a special peril attends
this truth ? It is like the rain which the Apostle
speaks of, which, if it does not make the earth bear

---

[1] Psalm l. 1, 9, 13, 14.   [2] St. Luke i. 32, 35, 76.

[3] St. Luke vi. 35.   [4] Acts x. 35.

fruit, cannot but stimulate a greater growth of thorns and briars.[1] If rightly received, it will increase our faith and hope in God, who though He is so high, spite of our fall, yet owns and claims us as His children. If abused, it may lead us to regard our fallen state as good, and so to consider the voice of our passions as the voice of God. The great coming apostasy will, if I err not, be the final perversion of this truth, when the last Antichrist, whose claim and boast will be a Divine humanity, will assume as man, in the fallen life of independence, that which can only be truly possessed by us, as partakers of the life of God, in Christ Jesus. There is therefore peril as well as blessing in the mystery of the " Most High," which, as we have seen, is so closely connected with the " priesthood after the order of Melchisedek." And yet, until we know this calling, and what we really are, we shall not understand the depth and fulness of God's purpose, and that, though fallen, man is a son of the " Most High."

And the way in which, both in the Old Testament and in the New, this name is joined with the other names, "Elohim " or " God," " Jehovah " or " LORD," and " El Shaddai " or " Almighty," shews that while some may abuse this truth, it is no less an integral part of the one harmonious whole of God's fulness, in which not only righteousness and love are one, but where also the election of some and the final salvation of all may both be seen as consistent parts of

[1] Heb. vi. 7, 8

one purpose. Thus the Psalmist in a single sentence speaks of the "secret of the Most High," of the "shadow of the Almighty," of the "refuge in Jehovah," and of the "trust in God." [1] For there is a "secret" in the "Most High," as to man's participation in the Divine nature, and the power of the "Most High" to abase him in the dust, if he abuse his gifts and calling, even though those "gifts and calling are without repentance." There is a "shadow of the Almighty;" a shadow in a double sense; either a cloud, with some darkness in the shadow, for there is pain both in self-judgment and in God's judgment; or a shadow, as the "shadow of a great rock in a weary land;" [2] for the "Almighty" is such a shadow also, "under which we may sit with great delight." [3] Such as know this can "say of Jehovah," who "judges evil," "He is my refuge and my fortress:" such can say of "God," who loves in virtue of relationship, "In Him will I trust." And the song of those whom St. John sees standing on the "sea of glass, having the harps of God," and who "have gotten the victory over the beast and over his image," is again little more than a triumphant repetition of these same names of God, as all subserving our salvation and deliverance; for they say, "Great and marvellous are thy ways, Lord, God, Almighty; just and true are thy ways, thou King (or "Most High") of nations. [4] Who shall not fear thee, O Lord, and

---

[1] Psalm xci. 1, 2.   [2] Isa. xxxii. 2.   [3] Cant. ii. 3.

[4] There is a question whether the true reading is "King of

glorify thy name? for all nations shall come and worship before thee, for thy judgments are made manifest." [1] This is the " song of Moses and of the Lamb." These are the names, full of light and love, which the Word, whether as Law or Gospel, opens to us.

And the Church on earth re-echoes the same. In her Communion Service, which, in this part at least, comes down to us unaltered almost from Apostolic days, once and again we are taught to repeat the same four names in union; first, when we say, " It is very meet, right, and our bounden duty, that we should at all times, and in all places, give thanks to thee, O Lord, Holy Father, Almighty, Everlasting God.   Therefore with angels and archangels, and with all the company of heaven, we laud and magnify thy glorious name, evermore praising thee, and saying, Holy, Holy, Holy, Lord, God of hosts: heaven and earth are full of thy glory: Glory be to thee, O Lord, Most High ; " and again, in the " Gloria in excelsis," where we say, " Glory be to God on high, and on earth peace, good will towards men.   We praise thee, we bless thee, we worship thee, we glorify thee, we give thanks to thee for thy

---

ages," or " King of nations."   Alford, in his text, adopts the reading, " King of nations," which is supported by a mass of MSS., and is given also in the margin of the Authorised Version; but in a note he adds, that " in the conflict of authorities it is impossible to decide " whether ἐθνῶν or αἰώνων was the original : the context seems to me to shew that it must have been ἐθνῶν.

[1] Rev. xv. 2, 4.

great glory, O Lord, God, heavenly King, God, the Father, Almighty. . . . For thou only art holy, thou only art the Lord, thou only, O Christ, with the Holy Ghost, art Most High, in the glory of God the Father."

Blessed for ever be the " LORD," " God," " Almighty," the " Most High," for such a revelation of Himself, that men may know and trust and joy in Him.

5

LORD OR ADONAI

THE names of God, which we have so far noticed, have mainly revealed His nature : " Elohim," His unchanging love ; " Jehovah," His righteousness and truth ; " El Shaddai," that He is a giver or pourer out of Himself for others ; " El Elyon," that though Most High, He is yet of a kindred nature with us. The names which remain for our consideration speak rather of His relationships, to things or persons, whether in heaven or earth. Not that we can say of any view of God that it excludes the others, or that this or that name speaks only of His nature, while some other name dwells exclusively on His relationships. God's perfections are so united that we cannot know one without seeing in it something of all, though one may and does more prominently bring out one aspect, and another some other aspect, of His fulness. It is here as in the Four Gospels, where each differing view of our Lord contains or gives hints of all. Thus the names "Elohim," "Jehovah," "El Shaddai," and " El Elyon," though they do not exclude the relationships which are in God Himself, and in which He likewise stands both to His fallen and unfallen creatures, rather reveal this or that perfection of His nature ; while the names which follow, " Adonai," " El Olam," and " Jehovah Sabaoth," speak more directly of His relationships, either to men or angels, or to the differing and successive ages, in and through which He works His purposes. These latter, though in themselves not perhaps so wondrous as some of the preceding, may touch us more directly, as shewing what is becoming in those, who by grace are called to know God's mind, and to have such close and abiding relationships with the Lord and God of all.

The name which we are now to consider is " Adonai," which our Authorised Version translates " Lord,"—not by any means the same word as " LORD," which is the usual rendering of the name " Jehovah." [1] This name, " Adonai," is first found in Abram's address to God, when, after his interview with Melchisedek, " the word of Jehovah came to Abram in a vision, saying, Fear not, Abram : I am thy shield, and thy exceeding great reward ; and Abram said, Lord GOD, (that is " Adonai Jehovah,") what wilt thou give me, seeing I go childless ? " and again immediately after, when " Jehovah said, I am

---

[1] I have already said, in speaking of the name " Jehovah," that the Jews of old not only wrote the name " Jehovah," wherever it occurred alone in Scripture, with the vowel points of " Adonai," but actually read " Adonai " instead of " Johovah," except where, as in Genesis xv. 2, 8, and like places, the word " Adonai " is united with " Jehovah," in which cases they wrote " Jehovah" with the vowel points of " Elohim," and read " Elohim " for " Jehovah."

the LORD, that brought thee out of Ur of the
Chaldees, to give thee this land to inherit it: and
Abram said, Lord GOD, (that is " Adonai Jehovah,")
whereby shall I know that I shall inherit it?"[1]
Abram again uses the same name repeatedly in his
addresses to God, when he intercedes for Sodom;[2]
and it is, as we shall see, a name which is continually
in the mouth of all God's servants generation after
generation. The question is, or rather it is no
question, What does this name reveal? " Adonai "
is simply the plural of the Hebrew word, " Adon,"
which means " lord " or " master," and which both in
the singular and plural is constantly applied to God.[3]
When applied to man, as it constantly is, this word
is used to express two well-known earthly relationships; first, the relation of a master to his slave or
servant;[4] and then of that of a husband to his wife.[5]

---

[1] Gen. xv. 1–8.   [2] Gen. xviii. 27, 30, 31, 32.

[3] For the singular, " Adon," אדון, as used of God, see Exod.
xxiii. 17; xxxiv. 23; Joshua iii. 11, 13; Neh. viii. 10; Psalm viii. 1,
9; xcvii. 5; cxiv. 7; cxxxv. 5; cxlvii. 5; Isa. i. 24; iii. 1; x. 16;
and elsewhere. The plural, " Adonai," אדני, occurs, as a title of
God, in countless places. Gesenius says that " the י in אדני is
the ancient termination for ים, and this form of plural is used
exclusively of God, both when He is addressed or spoken of."
When the word in the plural is used of men or angels, as in Isa.
xxvi. 13; Jer. xxvii. 4; Amos iv. 1; Psalm cxxxvi. 3; Prov. xxv.
13; and similar passages; the usual plural termination, ים, is
used. (*Heb. Lex.* on the word.)

[4] Gen. xxiv. 9, 10, 12, 14, 27, 35, &c.; xxxix. 2, 3, 7, 8; Exod.
xxi. 4, 5, 6; Judges xix. 11; and in many other places.

[5] Gen. xviii. 12; Judges xix. 27; 1 Kings i. 17, 18; Psalm
xlv. 11; 1 St. Peter iii. 6; &c.

To see its meaning as applied to God, we have only
to understand what these relationships exactly were,
which God has chosen to express His relations towards us.

Of old both slave and wife occupied a position
somewhat different from that which is accorded to
wives and servants at the present day. The title,
" Adon," or " Lord," whether as meaning " master "
or " husband," expressed a personal relationship,
which involved rights of lordship and possession.
The slave or wife were "not their own." [1] Both,
voluntarily or involuntarily, belonged to, and were the
property of, their lord.   In the slave the relationship
was binding quite irrespective of his own will.   As a
rule he or his parents were either purchased for money,
or were captives taken from an enemy; [2] for in those
days there were but two ways of dealing with captives
in war, namely, either putting them to death, or re-
ducing them to slavery.   In the case of the wife,
though she too generally was given or sold by her
father,[3] there might be more of the element of free
will; for the woman, as we see in Rebekah's case,
might be asked, " Wilt thou go with this man ? " [4]
But, once a man's wife, she was his for life, unless she
should be put away for some evil in her, or for unfaithfulness.[5]   With their will however, or without it, slave
or wife stood in a relation of subjection to their lord,

---

[1] 1 Cor. vi. 19, 20.   [2] Lev. xxv. 44–46.   Numb. xxxi. 35.
[3] Gen. xxviii. 15–20 ; Exod. xxi. 7–11.
[4] Gen. xxiv. 58.   [5] Deut. xxiv. 1.

where faithfulness received due honour and reward, while unfaithfulness would no less surely be visited with just judgment.

Now the name " Adonai," or " Lord," teaches that a relationship answering to that of servants to their lord, and of wives to their husbands, exists between God in heaven and His creature man upon the earth. Not only do the elect, in their approaches to Him, constantly use this name in addressing God, to express their relation to and dependence on Him, as well as their faith in the faithfulness of One, who, because He is their rightful Lord, is bound to sustain, and keep, and help them; but God also no less, when speaking of Himself, continually claims this title,[1] as declaring His relationships of Master and Husband to us,—relationships, which, while they set us in the place of honour, for to be even a servant, much more to be the beloved, of the " King of kings " is great honour, no less involve most solemn responsibilities, if, called with such a calling, we are unfaithful to it. In nothing more therefore than in the confession or denial of this name do we see the radical contrast between the Church and the world. The Church is Church because it acknowledges relationship:[2] the world is world because in practice it denies it. The great mark of the elect is that they " know the LORD,"[3]

---

[1] See Isa. viii. 7; Job xxviii. 28; and in countless other places.

[2] The English word, "Church," an abridgment or corruption of the Greek word κυριακή, simply means "belonging to the Lord."

[3] 1 Sam. iii. 7; Jer. ix. 24; xxiv. 7; xxxi. 34; St. John xvii. 3.

while the world yet knows Him not,[1] and acts as
far as may be in independence of Him. The world's
way is to do as it likes, think as it likes, speak as
it likes, without regard to any higher will above
it. Its great ones do "according to their will."[2]
They say, "Our lips are our own : who is lord over
us ?"[3] They live as if they were their own. All
obedience with such seems more or less degrading.
The very opposite marks all God's saints. All own
a Lord. All say, "Lord, what wilt thou have me to
do ?"[4] All with Christ, their Master, come to do,
not their own will, but the will of Him that sent
them ; for they know that not in self-will, but in
God's will, and in it alone, is perfect rest. Let us look
briefly at some of the teaching of Holy Scripture upon
this point, though indeed the lesson is so clear and so oft
repeated, that it hardly needs exposition or illustration.

First then to look at the name, "Adonai," as expressing the relationship of Master. Not one only,
but all God's saints, in trial of all kinds, turn instinctively to this name, as assuring them of the help
which they must require and will receive in their
appointed service. "Who goeth a warfare at his
own charges ?"[5] Who serveth a master at his
own cost ? "The eyes of servants look unto the
hand of their masters;"[6] and God's servants are no
less cared for. As not their own, but purchased by
their Lord, they are parts of His household in a way

---

[1] St. John viii. 19, 55 ; xvii. 25 ; Acts xvii. 23 ; 1 Cor. i. 21 ;
2 Thess. i. 8.

[2] Dan. viii. 4; xi. 3, 16, 36.   [3] Psalm xii. 4.

[4] Acts ix. 6.   [5] 1 Cor. ix. 7.   [6] Psalm cxxiii. 2.

no hired servant can be. For, strange as it may
seem to our modern views, the purchased slave of old
stood in a nearer relation to his lord than the hired
servant, who, as he worked for wages, could come or
go according to his own will. For the hired servant
might not eat of the Passover or of the holy things
of his master's house, while the purchased slave, as
belonging to his lord, was free of both these privileges.[1] Abram, the father of the faithful, in the
scene where the name " Adonai " first meets us, shews
how blessed is the relationship which he confesses
when he says, " My Lord," and " Lord GOD." For
at the time two burdens were pressing on his heart.
A seed and an inheritance had been promised him ;
and years had passed, and he was still childless and
without the promised land. But because in his
" Lord " he has One who cannot fail, he pours out
his complaint, saying, " Lord (Adonai) GOD, what
wilt thou give me ? " and again, " Adonai GOD, whereby
shall I know that I shall inherit it ? " and receives in
vision once and again enlarged assurances, that both
seed and inheritance, far larger than he hoped, shall
surely be given to him by his Lord : a seed even as the
stars of heaven for multitude, and for an inheritance
the land of many nations. He is yet but a servant :
he calls himself a " slave : "[2] but on his " Lord's "
faithfulness and power he relies for everything.

It is so with all God's servants. Their sufficiency

---

[1] Exod. xii. 45 ; Lev. xxii. 10, 11.

[2] Heb. עבד. See Gen. xviii. 3, 5 ; and elsewhere.

is in their Lord,[1] who fits each specially for the varied work committed to them. So Moses, called to bear God's message to Israel, says, " O my Lord, (Adonai,) I am not eloquent, neither before nor since thou hast spoken to thy servant. And the LORD said unto him, Who hath made man's mouth ? or who maketh the dumb, or deaf, or the seeing, or the blind ? Have not I, the LORD ? Now therefore go, and I will be with thy mouth, and will teach thee what thou shalt say." [2] So again, Joshua, when he is appointed to lead God's people into the land, and they are smitten at the outset by the men of Ai, turns to this name, saying, " O Lord, (Adonai,) what shall I say, when Israel turneth their backs before their enemies ? " and at once receives directions how he may discover the " accursed thing," which, though hidden, has been the cause of the defeat of God's people.[3] So again Gideon, when he is called to deliver Israel from the Midianites, and answers, " O my Lord, (Adonai,) why is all this befallen us ? " and again, " O my Lord, (Adonai,) wherewith shall I save Israel ? behold, my family is poor in Manasseh, and I am least in my father's house," receives for answer these words,—" Surely I will be with thee : go in this thy might : have not I sent thee ? " [4] The servant's strength is in his Lord. All God's servants prove this. Those in whom God's power has most been seen most freely confess it. Manoah childless ; [5]

---

[1] 2 Cor. iii. 5, 6. [2] Exod. iv. 10. [3] Josh. vii. 7, 8.
[4] Judges vi. 13-16. [5] Judges xiii. 8.

Samson in his bonds ; [1] Samuel in his youth with
Eli,[2] above all David, so greatly tried ; all confess
this name " Adonai," as their encouragement and
hope in every weakness. It seems as if David could
not too often repeat this name :—" Then went David
in, and said, Who am I, O Adonai Jehovah, and
what is my house, that thou hast brought me
hitherto ? And this was yet a small thing in thy
sight, O Adonai Jehovah ; but thou hast spoken also
of thy servant's house for a great while to come ;
and is this the manner of man, O Adonai Jehovah ?
And what can David say more unto thee ? for thou,
Adonai Jehovah, knowest thy servant. For thy
word's sake, and according to thine own heart, hast
thou done all these great things, to make thy servant
know them." [3] The Psalms continually repeat this
language :—" O LORD, our Lord, (Adonai,) how excellent is thy name in all the earth." Thy servants
are weak, but Thou art their " Lord." Therefore
even " out of the mouths of babes and sucklings
hast thou ordained strength. . . . What is man that
thou art mindful of him ? Man is like to vanity :
his days are as a shadow that passeth away. But
thou, O LORD, our Lord, hast put all things under
his feet. . . . O LORD, our Lord, how excellent is thy
name in all the earth." [4]

---

[1] Judges xvi. 28. [2] 1 Sam. iii. 9, 10.

[3] 2 Sam. vii. 18–21. We find the same constant repetition
of this name " Adonai " in Daniel's prayer, Dan. ix. 3–19.

[4] Psalm viii. 1–9 ; cxliv. 3, 4. See also Psalm xxxv. 23 ;
xxxviii. 9, 15, 22 ; xxxix. 7 ; xl. 17 ; li. 15 ; lxviii. 17, 19, &c.

The prophets still more bring out the blessings
which lie hid in the relationship which is confessed
under the name " Adonai." From or in connexion
with it, they draw their inspiration. To take one
or two examples out of many. It is the vision of
" Adonai," and of the service which is rendered Him
by heavenly hosts, which moves Isaiah, when all
things around him seem dark, to say, " Here am I :
send me."[1] He thus describes his call :—" In the
year that King Uzziah died, I saw the Lord,
(Adonai,) sitting upon his throne, high and lifted
up." The earthly lord is taken away. Signs are
abroad that for Israel's sins even the semblance of
power may ere long pass away from God's elect.
But the prophet's eye is opened to see a " Lord,"
who is yet " high and lifted up," and whose " train
filled the temple."   " Before Him stood the seraphim : each one had six wings; with twain he
covered his face, and with twain he covered his feet,
and with twain he did fly ; and one cried to another,
saying, Holy, Holy, Holy, is the LORD of Hosts : the
whole earth is full of His glory ; " all revealing, not
only the shrinking from self-display, which marks
the spirits nearest to the throne, but no less their
power and readiness to go anywhere to fulfil their
Lord's bidding. The immediate result of such a
vision is to make the prophet cry, " Woe is me, for
I am undone ; for I am a man of unclean lips," till
" there flew one of the seraphim, having a live coal

[1] Isa. vi. 1–8.

which he had taken from off the altar," the touch of
which upon the prophet's lips, not only imparted
new power, but also purged away his sin. And then
he " heard the voice of the Lord, (Adonai,) saying,
Whom shall I send, and who will go for us ? " What
could he say, but, that which all who have seen such
a vision always must say, " Here am I: send me."
With such a Lord, and with such help, and with
such hosts to serve His servants, who can refuse to
bear their Lord's message, whatever the cost of its
delivery.

The same name meets us in the mission of the
other prophets. In none perhaps do we more
clearly see its special import than in the call of
Jeremiah. Here was a man by nature timid, whose
words and ways constantly reveal even a womanly
tenderness and susceptibility. In his case it was no
natural self-confidence or self-conceit which brought
him out before his king and people as a prophet of
the LORD. More even than Moses he shrunk from
the burden laid upon him. But " the word of the
LORD comes to him," saying, " Before I formed thee
in the belly I knew thee ; and before thou camest
forth out of the womb I ordained thee a prophet to
the nations." And Jeremiah answered and said,
" Ah Lord (Adonai) GOD, behold I cannot speak, for
I am a child." But He answered, " Say not, I am a
child, for thou shalt go to all that I send thee, and
whatsoever I command thee thou shalt speak. Be
not afraid, for I am with thee." And then He

touched his mouth and said, "Behold, I have put my words in thy mouth. See, I have set thee this day over the nations, to root out, and to pull down, and to destroy, and to build, and to plant."[1]   It is the same in Ezekiel's case.   He, like Jeremiah, lived in evil days, when Israel was a "rebellious house,"[2] and the prophet with his people was "among the captives by the river Chebar." There "the heavens opened, and he saw visions of God." "The word of the LORD came to him,"[3] with a message from One, who claimed to be both his and Israel's "Lord," "whether they would hear, or whether they would forbear;" and who throughout the whole of this prophecy, more perhaps than in any other part of Holy Scripture, again and again repeats that He is "the Lord (Adonai) GOD,"[4] not of Israel only, but no less of the nations around, who have forgotten or denied that they too must be His servants.   "Other lords (Adonim) have had dominion" over God's elect, and over the world,[5] but God does not therefore surrender His rightful lordship over all.   His message whether to Israel,[6] or to Ammon, or Moab, or Edom,[7] or to Tyre or Egypt,[8] is always prefaced by His rightful title, "the Lord (Adonai) GOD."

---

[1] Jer. i. 2-10.   [2] Ezek. ii. 7, 8.   [3] Ezek. i. 1, 3.

[4] Ezek. ii. 4. This name, "Adonai GOD," is used in more than two hundred other places in this one prophecy.

[5] Isa. xxvi. 13.

[6] Ezek. ii. 4 ; iii. 11, 27 ; v. 7, 8, 11 ; vi. 3, 11 ; vii. 2, 5, &c.

[7] Ezek. xxv. 3, 6, 7, 8, 12, 13.

[8] Ezek. xxvi. 3, 5, 15 ; xxviii. 3 ; xxix. 3, 8, 13, &c.

It is in the Gospels however above all that the import of this title is brought out most fully. For not until the Lord Himself came in the flesh, and "took the form of a servant,"[1] and had his "ear bored" to seal His service,[2] was the full blessing of this relationship revealed. Till then, so deeply had men fallen, all service was counted more or less a disgrace and badge of inferiority. God was serving all; feeding even ravens, clothing lilies, opening His hand to satisfy the desire of every living thing.[3] But men perceived it not. So the Lord of all revealed Himself in the service of Him who was His image, saying, "Behold my Servant, whom I uphold; mine elect, in whom my soul delighteth : I have put my Spirit upon Him, and He shall shew judgment to the Gentiles. He shall not strive nor cry, neither shall any man hear His voice in the streets. A bruised reed shall He not break, and smoking flax shall He not quench. He shall not fail nor be discouraged, till He have set judgment in the earth."[4] He was among us "as One that serveth,"[5] revealing, as till then it had never been revealed, the blessedness of subjection to our true and heavenly Lord, which not only gives man what he needs, a Master, to "uphold and put His Spirit on us," but which makes selfish fallen men, even if they know it not, conformed in some measure to Him, who, like a shepherd, can rule

---

[1] Phil. ii. 7. [2] Exod. xxi. 6 ; Psalm xl. 6 ; and Heb. x. 5.

[3] Psalm cxlv. 16 ; cxlvii. 9 ; St. Luke xii. 24, 27.

[4] Isa. xlii. 1–4 ; St. Matt. xii. 17–20. [5] St. Luke xxii. 27.

and govern, because He serves, all. None have ever spoken of service like the Lord. The Gospel which is devoted to witness of His Lordship shews this. Hear Him saying, " The disciple is not above his Master, nor the servant above his Lord : it is enough for the disciple that he be as his Master, and the servant as his Lord." [1] " Whosoever therefore will be great among you, let him be your minister, and whosoever will be chief among you, let him be your servant; even as the Son of Man came not to be ministered unto, but to minister, and to give His life a ransom for many." [2] " Blessed are those servants, whom the Lord when He cometh shall find watching. Verily I say unto you, that He shall gird Himself, and make them to sit down to meat, and will come forth and serve them." [3] The approval of faithful service is the same in the use of ten talents or of one. " Well done, good servant : thou hast been faithful over a few things. Enter thou into the joy of thy Lord." [4] Well may all the saints rejoice in the relationship, that God is indeed their " Lord," and that, with all their weakness, they may say with Paul, " His I am, and Him I serve." [5]

But the name " Adonai " reveals another even more blessed relationship. The title " Lord " is used, not of Master only, but of Husband. It tells, that,

---

[1] St. Matt. x. 24, 25. [2] St. Matt. xx. 26–28.
[3] St. Luke xii. 37. [4] St. Matt. xxv. 19–23.
[5] Acts xxvii. 23.

weak and fallen as we are, the Lord of all calls us
to the closest and most endearing communion with
Himself; to be "no more twain," but "joined to the
Lord," and "one spirit;"[1] that as a wife is not her
own, but her husband's, so we too are "not our own,"
but both in body and spirit are the Lord's.[2] The
language of Holy Scripture upon this point is such
as could never have entered into the heart of men,
had they not been possessed and taught by God's
Spirit. Take the words to Israel, the appointed
figure of God's elect:—"Thus saith the LORD, I
remember thee, the kindness of thy youth, the love of
thine espousals, when thou wentest after me in a land
that was not sown."[3] "Thy Maker is thy husband."[4]
"I am married to you, saith the LORD;"[5] and again,
"I was a husband unto them."[6] "Thus saith the
Lord (Adonai) GOD; . . . I made thee to multiply:
thy breasts are fashioned, and thine hair is grown.
Now when I passed by thee, and looked upon thee,
behold, thy time was the time of love, and I spread
my skirt over thee, and covered thy nakedness; yea,
I sware unto thee, and entered into a covenant with
thee, saith the Lord (Adonai) GOD, and thou be-
camest mine. And I clothed thee with broidered
work, and shod thee with badgers' skin, and I girded
thee about with fine linen, and I covered thee with
silk; I decked thee also with ornaments, and I put

---

[1] St. Matt. xix. 5, 6; 1 Cor. vi. 17.   [2] 1 Cor. vi. 19.

[3] Jer. ii. 2.   [4] Isa. liv. 5.

[5] Jer. iii. 14.   [6] Jer. xxxi. 32.

bracelets upon thy hands, and a chain about thy
neck; and I put a jewel on thy forehead, and ear-
rings in thine ears, and a beautiful crown upon thy
head.   Thus wast thou decked with gold and silver;
and thou didst eat fine flour, and honey, and oil;
and thou wast exceeding beautiful through my
beauty, which I had put upon thee, saith the Lord
(Adonai) God."[1]

Words like these are common to the prophets,
revealing something of that love, wherewith the
Lord has loved us, in giving Himself to us, that we
may give ourselves to Him for ever.   For to us too
the words are spoken, " Hearken, O daughter, and
consider : forget thine own people and thy father's
house; so shall the King greatly desire thy beauty,
for He is thy Lord, (Adonai,) and worship thou Him."[2]
Language fails to express the unutterable preciousness
of such a relationship, and the unspeakable blessings
which it pledges to those who accept it, and by grace
are faithful to it.   For it is not only certain gifts
which come upon the " beloved of the Lord; "[3] but
in the relationship itself, as " married to Him," provision is made to meet our folly, so long as, spite of
all our weakness, we are faithful to Him.   What for
instance can be more blessed than the law respecting
a woman's vows, " if she have a husband," and is
living with him.   Though in her folly she may " bind
her soul with any vow, if her husband disallows her on

---

[1] Ezek. xvi. 7–14.   [2] Psalm xlv. 10, 11.
[3] Deut. xxxiii. 12; Jer xxxi. 3.

the day he hears it, then he shall make her vows, wherewith she hath bound her soul, of none effect : her husband hath disallowed it, and the LORD shall forgive her." [1] Her foolish purpose " shall not stand." It is by grace " forgiven " in virtue of the will of him to whom she stands so closely related. " But every vow of a widow, or of her that is divorced, wherewith they have bound their souls shall stand ; " [2] for with those who have been put away for their unfaithfulness, or, having been united to that which is dead, are without their " head,"—for " the husband is the head of the wife," [3]—there is no " Lord " to set aside and disallow their folly, and thus their foolish purpose " binds their souls."

The Song of Songs from first to last is the appointed witness of the delight, which both lover and beloved draw from this most intimate of all relationships. The earthly joy shadows the heavenly. For if all creatures are voices, silently witnessing to us of Him who is the great Archetype,—if sun and air, and bread and wine, lilies and cedars, sowing and reaping, all are telling something of the glory and fulness of Him, who is Himself our Lord, our Refuge, and our Portion,[4]—much more must man, who is God's image,[5] in that which most marks him, that is in his love for one above all others, shadow forth that Highest Love, which of twain makes one, and thus fills both with gladness.   God at least does not shrink

---

[1] Numb. xxx. 6–8.   [2] Numb. xxx. 9.   [3] Eph. v. 23.
[4] Psalm xvi. 2, 5 ; cxix. 57 ; cxlii. 5.   [5] 1 Cor. xi. 7.

from speaking of His joy in making us His own, and
in giving Himself to us as ours for ever. " All the
promises of God in Christ are in Him Yea, and in
Him Amen." [1]   And He hath said, " As a bridegroom
rejoiceth over the bride, so shall thy God rejoice over
thee." [2]   And the Song of Songs shews how the loved
one reciprocates this love, as she sings, "I am my
Beloved's, and His desire is toward me." [3]   Blessed
therefore as it is to know the Lord as " Master,"
it is as nothing to the joy of knowing the still
nearer relationship of " Husband," to which the name
"Adonai " calls us.   For, as one has said, while " work
is the result of one ruling or directing another, fruit is
only the result of a union between two." [4]   We may
do good work as servants, if we are obedient to our
Lord ; but to produce and bring forth the " new
man," which is His image, there must be that perfect
self-surrender, and union with Him, of which the
marriage bond is the appointed figure.   And we may
be espoused, while yet we are not married, to Him.[5]
But without union with our Lord we are, and must
be, barren.   Fruit, bearing His likeness, can never be
produced by any soul until it is perfectly the Lord's.

Such are some of the blessings which gather
round the name " Adonai," or " Lord : " such the
privileges of knowing God as " Master," and still more
as " Husband."   But for this very reason, because

---

[1] 2 Cor. i. 20.   [2] Isa. lxii. 5.   [3] Cant. vii. 10.

[4] Charles George Gordon, *Reflections in Palestine*, p. 74.

[5] Compare 2 Cor. xi. 2 ; and Rev. xix. 7.

these relationships are so intimate and full of mutual confidences,—for husbands must needs trust their wives, and masters their servants,—the least unfaithfulness in such relationships involves the greatest sin,—sin for which neither diligence, nor beauty, nor cleverness, can make the slightest compensation. In wife or servant perfect faithfulness is the first thing, and indispensable. And the more a soul is favoured, the greater the gifts entrusted to it, the closer its union with its Lord, whether as Master or as Husband, the greater is the sin of the very least and apparently most trifling unfaithfulness. An act which in a stranger might be nothing, in a trusted servant would be a crime: a look or word, or the lack of such, which would be unnoticed in those not related to us, in a loved wife might be unpardonable. Sins are relative. Hence such words as those of the prophet:—" You only have I known of all the families of the earth: therefore I will punish you for your iniquities." [1]   Times of ignorance God winks at or overlooks,[2] even as we overlook the faults of little children. Even unfaithfulness in those not trusted or nearly related to us does not greatly touch us. But evil in one's own house must be judged, if we would not be partakers in it. Hence, as the Lord's Supper teaches, communion involves judgment. If we can judge and correct ourselves, we are not judged of the Lord. If we do not correct ourselves, the nearer our relation to the Lord, the

---

[1] Amos iii. 2.   [2] Acts xvii. 30.

surer and sorer will be His judgment and correction.[1]

It is of this judgment, as well as of the blessings of nearness to the Lord, that the name " Adonai" is the special witness. For indeed blessings may be judgments, and must be, if we are unfaithful; even as judgments are blessings, for they are sent to bring souls out of their unfaithfulness. Therefore both to servant or wife, if faithless, " Adonai " must be judge. Need I quote the words of prophets, or of the Lord of prophets, to shew that the sin of His servants must bring its own judgment:—" Thus saith the LORD, If I be a Master, (Adon,) where is my fear? O priests that despise my name; and ye say, Wherein have we despised it? Ye offer polluted bread upon mine altar, and ye say, Wherein have we polluted thee? Ye offer the blind and the lame for sacrifice. Is it not evil? Offer it now to thy governor; will he be pleased with thee or accept thy person? saith the LORD of hosts. Who is there even among you that would shut the doors for nought? Neither do ye kindle fire upon mine altar for nought. I have no pleasure in you, saith the LORD of hosts; neither will I accept an offering at your hand. For ye said also, Behold what a weariness it is; and ye have snuffed at it, saith the LORD of hosts; and ye brought that which was torn, and the lame and the sick. Should I accept this at your hand? saith the LORD. Therefore now, O ye priests, this command-

[1] 1 Cor. xi. 31, 32.

ment is for you. If ye will not hear, and if ye will not lay it to heart, to give glory to my name, saith the LORD, I will even send a curse upon you, and I will curse your blessings : yea, I have cursed them already, because ye do not lay it to heart."[1] What judgment can be sorer, than that one's blessings should become a curse. And yet thus it must be with those, who, called to nearness to their Lord, are unfaithful to their high calling. We know Who it is that says,—" But and if that evil servant say in his heart, My Lord delayeth His coming, and shall begin to smite his fellow-servants, and to eat and drink and to be drunken, the Lord of that servant shall come in a day that he looketh not for him, and in an hour that he is not aware of, and shall cut him in sunder, and shall appoint him his portion with the hypocrites : there shall be weeping and gnashing of teeth. And that servant, which knew his Lord's will and prepared not himself, shall be beaten with many stripes ; but he that knew not, and did commit things worthy of stripes, shall be beaten with few stripes. For unto whomsoever much is given, of him shall much be required, and to whom men have committed much, of him they will ask the more."[2]

It is even worse with the unfaithful wife, though her husband's love remains unchanged. The prophets seem to labour under this burden when they would utter it :—" Surely as a wife treacherously departeth

[1] Mal. i. 6–12 ; and ii. 1, 2.

[2] St. Matt. xxiv. 48–51 ; and St. Luke xii. 45–48.

from her husband, so have ye dealt treacherously with me, O house of Israel, saith the LORD." [1] "Thine own wickedness shall correct thee, and thy backslidings shall reprove thee : know therefore and see that it is an evil thing and bitter, that thou hast forsaken the LORD thy God." [2] For " thou didst trust in thine own beauty, and playedst the harlot, and pouredst out thy fornication on every one that passed by. And it came to pass, after all thy wickedness, (woe, woe, unto thee, saith Adonai GOD,) that thou hast made thee a high place in every street. And thou hast not been as a harlot, in that thou scornest hire, but as a wife that committeth adultery, who taketh strangers instead of her husband. Wherefore, O harlot, hear the word of the LORD. Thus saith the Lord (Adonai) GOD, Because thy filthiness was poured forth, through thy whoredoms with thy lovers, and with all the idols of thine abominations ; therefore, behold, I will gather all thy lovers, with all whom thou hast loved, and them also that thou hast hated, and I will judge thee as women that break wedlock and that shed blood are judged, and I will give thee blood in fury and jealousy. And I will give thee into their hands, and they shall strip thee of thy clothes, and take thy fair jewels, and leave thee naked and bare ; and they shall execute judgments upon thee, and I will cause thee to cease from playing the harlot any more." [3]

---

[1] Jer. iii. 20.   [2] Jer. ii. 19.

[3] Ezek. xvi. 15–41.

And yet, because "Adonai" is God, even thus, and from all this, shall the fallen wife be saved at last by Him who first loved her :—" As I live, saith Adonai GOD, Sodom thy sister hath not done, she nor her daughters, as thou hast done, thou and thy daughters. Neither hath Samaria committed half thy sins. They are more righteous than thou. Yea, be thou confounded, in that thou hast justified thy sisters. Nevertheless I will remember my covenant with thee in the days of thy youth, and I will establish unto thee an everlasting covenant. Then shalt thou remember thy ways and be ashamed, when thou shalt receive thy sisters, thine elder and thy younger ; that thou mayest remember, and be confounded, and never open thy mouth any more because of thy shame, when I am pacified toward thee for all that thou hast done, saith the Lord (Adonai) GOD." [1] Well may saints and angels cry with wonder, " Holy, Holy, Holy, LORD " ! Who is like unto our " Master " and our " Lord " !

Such then is the relationship between the Creator and creature, which the name " Adonai," or " Lord," reveals to us. And though it falls far short of that still more wondrous vision, of the " Father " and the " Son," which is opened in the gospel, yet in the name " Master " and " Husband " we have enough, and more than enough, to make us " strong in the Lord," and

---

[1] Ezek. xvi. 60–63. See too Isa. i. 24–27, for similar words of threatening and promise from " Adonai."

to " rejoice in Him, alway." [1]　For if the servant of
a prophet, as his master was taken from him, could
cry, " My father, my father, the chariot of Israel,
and the horsemen thereof : " [2]—if even in a Syrian
slave of old there could be such confidence and love,
that the servant could call his lord, " Father," saying,
" My father, if the prophet had bid thee do some
great thing, wouldest thou not have done it ? " [3]—
what should be our faith and hope in Him, who
calls us His " servants," and His " beloved " ?　And
especially in these last days, when the spirit of
lawlessness is growing, and all the bonds which have
held society together seem in peril of being broken,
it is more than ever our wisdom to remember the
" Lord," " whose service is perfect freedom," and
whose love for His beloved " passeth knowledge."
Blessed be His name, the day is coming, when
" there shall be no more curse," but His " servants
shall do Him service, and shall see His face, and His
name shall be upon their foreheads." [4]　If we believe not, yet He abideth faithful : He cannot deny
Himself. [5]　He hateth putting away. [6]　His gifts
and calling are without repentance. [7]　Even unfaithful Israel shall obtain mercy. [8]　For thus saith
the LORD, " In that day thou shalt call me Ishi ;
(that is My husband ;) and shalt call me no more
Baali ; (that is, My lord ;) and I will betroth thee

---

[1] Eph. vi. 10; and Phil. iv. 4.　　[2] 2 Kings ii. 3, 12.
[3] 2 Kings v. 13.　　[4] Rev. xxii. 3, 4.　　[5] 2 Tim. ii. 13.
[6] Mal. ii. 16.　　[7] Rom. xi. 29.　　[8] Rom. xi. 31.

unto me for ever ; yea, I will betroth thee unto me in righteousness, and in judgment, and in loving kindness, and in mercies. And I will say to them which were not my people, Thou art my people; and they shall say, Thou art my God."[1] Oh, day of wonders, when "the marriage of the Lamb is come, and His Wife hath made herself ready."[2]

I conclude with the words of one who knew " Adonai," and who in the day of his trouble found in this name, and in the other names of God, which in his anguish seemed instinctively to rise upon his lips, that help and comfort which he had not in himself, and could not find in creatures. How many in every age have found comfort in the words :—" Will Adonai, (my Lord and Husband,) cast off for ever ? Will He be favourable no more ? Is His mercy clean gone for ever ? Doth His promise fail for evermore ? Hath Elohim, (who is in covenant with me), forgotten to be gracious ? Hath He in anger shut up His tender mercies ? And I said, This is my infirmity : but I will remember the years of the right hand of the Most High; (even of Him whose offspring we all are, even though as Gentiles we may have wandered from Him.) Yea, I will remember the works of Jah, (Jehovah, the righteous One, who gives Himself to be our righteousness;) surely I will remember thy wonders of old."[3] So cried a soul of old who knew " Adonai." Would to God that those to whom these names have been

---

[1] Hos. ii. 16–23.   [2] Rev. xix. 7.   [3] Psalm lxxvii. 7–11.

matter for self-exalting criticism, rather than for faith and hope in Him, who is only truly known as we obey Him, might be brought even by trouble to know themselves, and the grace of Him, who reveals His fulness to His creatures as they need it. They that know His name will put their trust in Him. And they that trust in Him shall never be confounded.

6

EVERLASTING GOD OR EL OLAM

THE next name of God in Holy Scripture is " El
Olam," which in our Authorised Version is translated
" Everlasting God," [1] a name but seldom repeated,
and which as yet has been little noticed even by
students of " the oracles of God," [2] but which reveals
a truth and fact, as to God's ways with fallen man,
shewing Him patient and wise as well as righteous
and all-loving. For this name tells us that God
reveals Himself to men by varying dispensations,
" at sundry times and in divers manners," [3] as they
can bear it; in all carrying out His one unchanging
purpose, to bring us out of our fall and make us
partakers of His own blessedness. We shall see, if
God permit, how this name reveals this truth ; though
the wisdom of His ways is still hidden from not a
few, who can yet bless Him that they are and shall
be His for ever.

This name, " El Olam," first meets us in Abram's
life, after his name is changed from Abram to

---

[1] Heb. אל עולם, literally, " God of the age." In the Septuagint, Θεὸς αἰώνιος. In the Vulgate, " Deus æternus."

[2] Rom. iii. 2.   [3] Heb. i. 1.

Abraham, when the man of faith, long barren, has received the heir of promise, Isaac, and, as a consequence, the bondmaid and her son are cast out. "At that time" the Gentile comes to Abraham, and a covenant is made with him at Beersheba, the "Well of the Oath," and "there Abraham called on the name of the LORD, the Everlasting God."[1] The truth which this name teaches therefore belongs to a certain stage in the life of faith, when the life of sonship, which Isaac figures, is brought forth by Sarah, that is the Gospel,[2] and the carnal seed, the fruit of law, is judged and cast out. For, as St. Paul teaches, all these are shadows of spiritual truths ; the birth of Isaac of the " free woman," and the rejection of the " son of the bondmaid," being appointed figures of the change from law to gospel. We do not know at first, that, in God's dealing with His elect, there may and will be diversities of operation and a change of dispensation ; and that though for a season law is needed, it must give place to gospel, and that grace itself will be succeeded by a fuller revelation of God's glory ; each varied stage being needed for man's perfecting. As we advance this opens to us, and we learn, that, precious as are the truths revealed under the names " Elohim," " Jehovah," " El Shaddai," or " Adonai," there is yet more to be revealed, full of instruction for us, if like Abraham we will still walk with God.

Now both the fact that in God's dealings with

[1] Gen. xxi. 10, 22, 33. [2] Gal. iv. 22, 30.

His creatures there are successive " times " or " ages "
or dispensations, and that this is a " mystery," or
" secret," which is only opened as we grow in grace, is
involved and taught in the name " El Olam." For
the word " Olam," which is rendered " Everlasting,"
contains in itself both the idea of a " secret," and
also of " time," or of " an age." The " El," which we
translate " God," here, as in the names " El Shaddai "
and " El Elyon," expresses " Power," [1] even the Power
of Him, " who doeth as He will in the armies of
heaven and among the inhabitants of the earth." [2]
The word " Olam " has two senses, though the connexion between the two is obvious. Its first and
original sense is to " *conceal*," or " *hide*," or something " *hidden*." [3] Hence it came to mean " *time
hidden from man*," or " *time indefinite*." In our Version
it is often translated " *for ever*," and in certain places
it may mean " time unmeasured," " for an age," or
" for ages." But that strictly speaking it expresses
a limited time is clear, not only from many passages

---

[1] See pp. 64, 65 above.   [2] Dan. iv. 35.

[3] See Lev. iv. 13 ; v. 2 ; xx. 4 ; 1 Sam. xii. 3 ; Psalm xc. 8
and many other places. In Eccl. iii. 11, it is still a question
how the word should be translated. Our Authorised Version
translates it " world," as it translates αἰών in St. Matt. xiii. 39,
and elsewhere : the Revised Version translates it " world," or
" eternity :" the Septuagint render it by αἰών : while Parkhurst
(see his *Lexicon*, on the word,) translates it " obscurity," reading
the whole verse as follows :—" He hath made everything beautiful
in its season, but He hath even put such *obscurity* (olam) in the
midst of them, that man cannot find out the work that God
doeth from beginning to end."

where the time referred to can only be a life-time, or
till the year of Jubilee, or for the period of the
Jewish dispensation, but from other passages, where
the word is redoubled or used in the plural, (which
it could not be if it meant "for ever,") where its
meaning is "for ages," or "from age to age." [1]   A
few examples of the varied uses of the word may shew
us its real force, and how it throws light upon the
name of God which we are now considering.

The word "Olam" then is used of a limited time
in the following places among many others, though
our Authorised Version in some of them has rendered
it "for ever ; " as for example, where we read of the
" Hebrew servant whose ear is bored," of whom it is
said, that " he should serve his master *for ever* ; " and
again where we have the law respecting the heathen
bondslaves, whom Israel shall possess, of whom it is
written, that " they shall be your bondmen *for ever* : "
in both which places the word can only mean " for
life," or " until the year of Jubilee." [2]   We find the
word again in Hannah's utterance, where she says,
" I will not go up until the child be weaned, and

---

[1] For instances of the plural use of the word, עלמים, see
Psalm lxxvii. 7, 8 ; Isa. xlv. 17 ; Dan. ix. 24, &c.

[2] Exod. xxi. 6 ; and Lev. xxv. 46.   In the former of these
passages the word is explained by Josephus, (*Antiqq.* iv. 8. § 28,)
and by the Rabbinists, (see the article on the word " Slave," in
Smith's *Dictionary of the Bible*, p. 1331,) to mean "*until the
year of Jubilee*," partly from the universality of the freedom then
proclaimed, and also because it was the duty of the servant, as a
free-born Israelite, then to resume the cultivation of his recovered inheritance.

then I will bring him, that he may appear before the Lord, and abide there *for ever* ; " words which she afterwards explains by saying, " *As long as he liveth*, he shall be lent unto the Lord." [1] So again Achish says of David, when he came to Gath, " He shall be my servant *for ever*." [2] The same word is sometimes simply translated " *time*," as in the law of redemption of inheritances, where we read, that " the houses in their cities the Levites may redeem at any " *time*." [3] It is also used in reference to the past, as in the words, " Your fathers dwelt on the other side of the flood *in old time* ; " [4] and again, " See, it hath been already *of old time* ; " [5] and again where the Lord by the prophet says to Tyre, " I will bring thee down to the pit with the people *of old time* ; " [6] and again, where the Psalmist says, " I remember the days of *old*." [7] We find a kindred use of the word where Isaiah says, " I have a long *time* holden my peace ; " [8] and again where the same prophet, speaking of the past, uses the plural form of the word, saying, " Awake, O arm of the Lord, as in the generations *of old*." [9] In one place the word is translated " *world*," as when the Psalmist says, " These are the ungodly who prosper in the *world*," [10] meaning " *in this present age*," or " *life-time*." In all these places the word, " Olam,"

---

[1] 1 Sam. i. 22, 28.   [2] 1 Sam. xxvii. 12.

[3] Lev. xxv. 32.   [4] Josh. xxiv. 2.

[5] Eccl. i. 10.   [6] Ezek. xxvi. 20.

[7] Psalm cxliii. 5. See too Gen. vi. 4 ; and Deut. xxxii. 7.

[8] Isa. xlii. 14.   [9] Isa. li. 9 : Heb. עֹלָמִים.

[10] Psalm lxxiii. 12.

simply expresses " time." It has no reference whatever to what we call eternity.

Still more abundant proof of the meaning of the word is to be found in its constant use respecting the period and appointments of the Jewish dispensation. For it is used of the Aaronic priesthood,[1] and of the office of the Levites,[2] and of the Passover,[3] and of the meat-offering,[4] and the Tabernacle service, and other ordinances of the old outward worship, which now is " done away,"[5] all of which in our Authorised Version are said to be "*for ever.*" The same word is used of the inheritance given to Caleb ; [6] of Ai being a desolation ; [7] of the punishment of Eli's house ; [8] and of the leprosy of Gehazi, of which it is said that it " shall cleave to him and to his seed *for ever.*"[9] So again, of the land of Canaan it is said, that " the seed of Abraham shall inherit it *for ever,*"[10] while the self-same word is repeated in the curse threatened upon Israel for their disobedience, as when we read, " These curses shall come on thee, and pursue thee, till thou be destroyed, and they shall be upon thee for a sign, and upon thy children *for ever.*"[11] In like manner of Ammon and Moab it is said, " Thou shalt not seek their peace *for ever* ; "[12] and again, " They shall not come into the congrega-

[1] Exod. xl. 15.   [2] 1 Chron. xv. 2.
[3] Exod. xii. 14, 17.   [4] Lev. vi. 18.
[5] 2 Cor. iii. 7.   [6] Josh. xiv. 9.
[7] Josh. viii. 28.   [8] 1 Sam. iii. 13, 14.
[9] 2 Kings v. 27.   [10] Gen. xiii. 15 ; Exod. xxxii. 16.
[11] Deut. xxviii. 45, 46.   [12] Deut. xxiii. 6.

tion of the Lord *for ever*."¹ These and countless similar uses of the word, "Olam," shew that it expresses "time," a "life-time" or an "age," but always speaks of some passing period, which runs its course and fulfils its purpose in God's dealings with the creature.

The question is, What is the exact meaning of the word when it is applied to God, as in the passage where it first occurs in Abraham's life, and in the other places where it occurs in Holy Scripture.² I answer, the name itself, if only literally translated, contains and gives the key to the mystery, which is revealed, yet hidden, in it. "El Olam" is the "Age-God," or "God of Ages,"³ that is, the God who works His will, not all at once, but through successive times and varied dispensations. For in the restoration of His fallen creatures there are stages. As "Jehovah," He is ever "I AM," the witness, not of past or future, but of the truth itself, which cannot pass, but is eternal. "El Olam" shews Him rather as the God of "times and seasons," in which He works to meet a fall, which prove that they are not the true life by "waxing old and vanishing away."⁴ Thus this

---

¹ Deut. xxiii. 3.

² See Psalm xc. 2 ; Isa. xl. 28 ; lxiii. 16 ; Jer. x. 10 ; Micah v. 2 ; Rom. xvi. 36 ; 1 Tim. i. 17, &c.

³ Dr. Robert Young, in his new translation of the Bible, renders the word "Olam," "*age-during*." See his version *passim*, e.g. Gen. xxi. 33 ; Exod. xii. 14, 17 ; xl. 14, &c. I should rather render it "*age-working*."

⁴ Heb. viii. 13. The following words of St. Augustine upon this point are so striking that I subjoin them. He says, "Any-

name foretells exactly what the Apostle Paul calls the "purpose of the ages,"[1] namely, that in His dealings with men for their salvation, while His purpose remains absolutely unchanged, God yet reveals Himself in varying degrees, according to man's capacity to receive the growing revelation; first in the flesh, then in the Spirit; now giving law, now gospel; at one time with an election, at another with a call to all people. In a word this name "El Olam" teaches, that in the restoration and redemption of mankind there is an appointed order, a first and a last, both component parts of one purpose, and that these "times" and "times of times," some past, some future, are the direct working of the "King of ages, the only wise God,"[2] who thus reveals the "manifold wisdom," and "unsearchable riches," of His only-begotten Son.[3]

---

thing whatever hath not true being, if it change. If that is not which was, a kind of death hath taken place. Something is made away with there, that was, and now is not. Something is changed, and is, that formerly was not. O Truth, Thou only art. For in all the movings of the creature I find two times, past and future. I seek the present. Nothing stayeth. . . . Past and future I find in all the motion of things. In the Truth which abideth I find not past and future, but only present, and this without fear or possibility of change. Take point by point the mutations of things. Thou wilt find *Hath been* and *Will be.* Take God, and thou wilt find *I am*, where *Hath been* and *Will be* cannot be."—*Tractat. in Johan.* xxxviii. § 10.

[1] Eph. iii. 10, 11.

[2] 1 Tim. i. 17. Gr. τῷ βασιλεῖ τῶν αἰώνων.

[3] Eph. iii. 8, 10, 11. I may observe here that the title of our Lord, in Isaiah ix. 6, אֲבִי־עַד, which our Authorised Version translates, "Everlasting Father," is literally, the "Father of the age,"

Let us notice some of the illustrations which Holy Scripture gives us of this " purpose of the ages," first as it is set before us under the shadow of the law, and then as it is more clearly opened in the writings of the New Testament.

No one I think can have studied the complex appointments of the Mosaic law, without feeling, that, if all this ceremonial came from God, there must be some hidden wisdom, not only in what is commanded as to offerings and priesthood, but no less in the varied times and seasons, which are ordained for successive cleansings and redemptions, whether of persons or their lost inheritance, and in the law respecting the First-fruits and the First-born. Some of these are so remarkable that we can scarcely conceive that they can have been appointed without a purpose. But we are not left in doubt upon this point. The New Testament distinctly teaches that all these things are " shadows of good things to come," [1] and that in them God is revealing the way of man's return to Him, and the varied steps and times through which it is accomplished. I need not here speak of the " offerings " and " priesthood," for

---

with direct reference to the " age " or " dispensation " spoken of. Bishop Louth's note here is as follows :—" The Septuagint render the words, Πατὴρ μέλλοντος αἰῶνος, i.e., ' the Father of the world to come,' and the Vulgar Latin follow this translation." The Bishop adds, " I am persuaded it is from the authority of this text, that the Kingdom of the Messiah is called in the New Testament by the title of ' *the age* (or world) *to come.* "

[1] Col. ii. 17 ; and Heb. x. 1.

these only indirectly bear upon the name " El Olam."
It will be enough to shew how the "times" and
" seasons " of the law are the shadows of those
" ages," through which God works, and in virtue of
which He is the " God and King of ages."

I have spoken so fully on this point elsewhere,[1]
that I can hardly avoid some repetition here; but the
subject is so important, and so little understood, that
it will bear some repetition. Observe then how in
the law both cleansing and redemption in differing
cases take effect at different times. I refer to those
mystic periods of "seven days," [2] "seven weeks," [3]
" seven months," [4] " seven years," [5] and the " seven
times seven years," [6] which last complete the Jubilee,
all which are differing times for cleansing and deliverance. In the case of the leper, and of him
that was unclean by the dead, there were varied
times and stages of purification.[7] In the purification of the woman, if a son was born, her cleansing
was complete at the end of forty days : if she bore
a female child, not till twice forty.[8] In some cases
the debtor or bondman might go free at the return
of the Sabbatic year : [9] in other cases not until the
year of Jubilee.[10] So again, if the next of kin re-

---

[1] In my volume on the *Restitution of all Things*, pp. 30-68.

[2] Lev. xii. 2 ; xiii. 5, 21, 26 ; xiv. 8, &c.

[3] Lev. xxiii. 15.   [4] Lev. xvi. 29 ; xxiii. 24.

[5] Lev. xxv. 4; Deut. xv. 9, 12.   [6] Lev. xxv. 8, 9.

[7] Lev. xiii. and xiv. ; and Numb. xix. 12.

[8] Lev. xii. 1-5.   [9] Exod. xxi. 2.

[10] Lev. xxv. 39, 40.

deemed the lost inheritance, it might be regained at once.[1] If this was not done, and the inheritance had been sold, it was lost until the year of Jubilee.[2] More striking still are the varied seasons, which are entitled "Feasts of the Lord,"[3] when the fruits which are brought forth out of the earth are gathered in due order: first, the sheaf or handful of unleavened ears, the first to spring up out of the dark earth, which lay the shortest time under its darkness, soonest ripe to be a sacrifice on God's altar, was offered at the first great Feast, which is the Passover:[4] then, fifty days later, the leavened cakes, offered at the Feast of Weeks, that is at Pentecost:[5] and lastly, in the seventh month, the Feast of Tabernacles, or of Ingathering, "in the end of the year, when all the field is gathered in."[6] In all these Feasts the seed of nature figures the seed of grace, and the first-fruits of the one are but a shadow of the other; that "seed of the kingdom," which is "not quickened except it die," and which returns to Him who made it, "every man in his own order; Christ the first-fruits; then they that are Christ's; after which cometh the end," when it shall be seen, that, as "the first-fruit is holy, the lump is also holy;"[7] according to the working whereby He is able to

---

[1] Lev. xxv. 25–27.

[2] Lev. xxv. 28.   [3] Lev. xxiii. 2, &c.

[4] Lev. xxiii. 10, 11; and St. Luke xxii. 1.

[5] Lev. xxiii. 17.

[6] Exod. xxiii. 16 Lev. xxiii. 39; Deut. xvi. 13.

[7] 1 Cor. xv. 22–28; Rom. xi. 16.

subdue all things unto Himself. I do not here attempt to explain all this. I have done so elsewhere. And this mystery of the "ages" is a "secret." I only say, these "times and seasons" all speak of better things, and are the divinely appointed witnesses of the great truth which is set before us in the name "El Olam," the "Everlasting God."

But even creation, in its varied stages, tells us the same story. In it "the Age-working God, the LORD, the Creator of the ends of the earth," [1] works, not in one act, but by degrees, and through successive and appointed days or seasons. In creation each day has its own work, to bring back some part of the fallen creature, and one part before another, from emptiness and confusion, to light and form and order. Six days of labour precede the day of rest. All things do not appear at once. Much is unchanged after "light," and a "heaven," are formed upon the first and second days.[2] But these first works act on all the rest, for both the "light" and "heaven" are fellow-workers with God's word in all the change that follows, till "all is very good." The Patriarchal lives even more clearly foretell the same mystery. There is a time when God still bears with the old world, though "the earth is filled with violence," [3] and a time when that world is judged by a flood, and a new earth emerges from the waters. There is a time when Hagar, the bondmaid, and a fleshly seed, have their permitted

---

[1] Isa. xl. 28.　　　[2] Gen. i. 4–8.　　　[3] Gen. vi. 11.

place in the elect house, and a time when "that which is born after the flesh" is cast out, to make way for that which is " born after the Spirit." [1] There is a time for the " sons of Levi " to " take tithes of the people according to the law," and a time for the " priesthood after the order of Melchisedek." [2] There is a time when Joseph is rejected by his brethren, and sold into Egypt, and a time when he is exalted to be head over the kingdom, and his brethren are brought to know and worship him. The prophets are full of the same teaching; of an " old covenant, which decayeth and waxeth old," and of a " new one, which is established upon better promises ; " [3] of the calling of Israel out of the nations, to be " as the firstripe in the fig tree at her first time," [4] and then of the " earth full of the knowledge of the LORD, as the waters cover the sea ; " [5] of the " time, times, and half a time," [6] while God's elect are tried, and of the " seventy weeks,"the decade of Jubilees, which " are determined to finish the transgression, and to make an end of sins, and to bring in everlasting righteousness." [7] All these are shadows of the " purpose of the ages," " which from the beginning of the world hath been hid in God," all whose ways are wisdom, even if men discern it not.

---

[1] Gal. iv. 22–30.

[2] Heb. vii. 5, 9.

[3] Jer. xxxi. 31–34 ; and Heb. viii. 6–8.

[4] Hos. ix. 10.

[5] Isa. xi. 9.

[6] Dan. xii. 7 ; and Rev. xii. 14.

[7] Lev. xxv. 8 ; Dan. ix. 24 ; and compare St. Matt. xviii. 22.

But even if we were without these figures, the
language of the New Testament, in its use of the
words, which our translators have rendered " for
ever " and " for ever and ever," [1] but which are literally " for the age," or " for the ages of ages," points
not uncertainly to the great truth taught by the name,
" El Olam," or " Age-working God," though as yet
the glad tidings of the " ages to come " have been
little opened.   The Epistles of St. Paul shew that the
" ages " are periods in which God is gradually working out a purpose, which was ordained in Christ
before the fall, and before those " age-times," [2] in and
through which the fall is being remedied.   So we
read, that " God's wisdom was ordained before the
ages to our glory ; " [3] that is, that God had a purpose
" before the ages," out of the very fall to bring
greater glory both to Himself, and to His fallen
creature.   Then we are told distinctly of the " purpose of the ages ; " [4] shewing that the work of renewal
would only be accomplished through successive ages.
Then we read, that " by the Son, God made the ages ; " [5]
for it was by what the Eternal Word uttered and revealed of God's mind in each successive age, that
each such age became what it distinctly was ; each

---

[1] Gr. εἰς αἰῶνα, and εἰς αἰῶνας αἰώνων.

[2] Gr. χρόνοι αἰώνιοι : 2 Tim. i. 9 ; Tit. i. 2.

[3] 1 Cor. ii. 7 ; πρὸ τῶν αἰώνων.

[4] Eph. iii. 11 : κατὰ πρόθεσιν τῶν αἰώνων, translated in our
Authorised Version, " the eternal purpose."   The Revised Version
gives the exact translation, in the margin.

[5] Heb. i. 2 ; and xi. 3.

age, like each day of creation, being different from
another by the form and measure in which the Word
of God was uttered in it, and therefore also by the
work effected in it, the work in each successive age,
as in the different days of creation, being wrought
first in one part, then in another, of the lapsed
creation. Then again we read of the "mystery
which has been hidden from the ages," [1] and again,
that the "mystery," (for he repeats the words,) "which
hath been hid from ages and generations, is now made
manifest to the saints, to whom God hath willed to
make known what is the riches of the glory of this
mystery, which is Christ in you, the hope of glory." [2]
In another place the Apostle speaks of "glory to God
in the Church by Christ Jesus, unto all generations
of the age of ages." [3] He further says, that Christ is
set " far above all principality and power, and every
name that is named, not only in this age, but in the
coming one; " [4] and again, that "now once in the
end of the ages He hath appeared, to put away sin
by the sacrifice of Himself; " [5] and that " on us the
ends of the ages are met; " [6] words which plainly
speak of some of the ages as past, and seem to imply
that other ages are approaching their consummation.
Lastly, he speaks of " the ages to come," in which

---

[1] Eph. iii. 9.   [2] Col. i. 26.

[3] Eph. iii. 21 : εἰς πάσας τὰς γενεὰς τοῦ αἰῶνος τῶν αἰώνων.

[4] Eph. i. 21.

[5] Heb. ix. 26 : ἐπὶ συντελείᾳ τῶν αἰώνων.

[6] 1 Cor. x. 11 : τὰ τέλη τῶν αἰώνων κατήντησεν.

God will " shew the exceeding riches of His grace in
His kindness toward us through Christ Jesus." [1]

It is of this " purpose of the ages," that the name
" El Olam " is the witness, telling of those " times of
refreshing from the presence of the Lord, when He
shall send Jesus Christ, who before was preached," [2]
and when, in due order, through righteous judgment,
cleansing, liberty, and rest, will be obtained by those
who are yet in bondage, and unclean, and without
their rightful inheritance.   In the " ages," and in no
other mystery of the gospel, do we find those " good
things to come," of which the legal " times and
seasons " were the shadow.   The " ages," like the
days of creation, speak of a prior fall : they are the
" times " through which God works, because there is
evil, and His rest is broken by it, but which have an
end when the work appointed to be done in them has
been accomplished, when all again is " very good."
God's perfect rest is not in the " ages," but beyond
them, when the mediatorial kingdom, which is " for
the ages of ages," [3] is " delivered up," [4] and Christ, by
whom all things are wrought in the ages, goes back to
the glory which He had " before the age times." [5]   And

---

[1] Eph. ii. 4–17. I may add here that in all the following
passages, *αἰών*, which is the Greek equivalent of the Hebrew
עולם, is used for this present or some other limited age or dispensation :—St. Matt. xii. 32 ; xiii. 39, 40; xxiv. 3 ; St. Luke xvi. 8 ;
xx. 34, 35 ; Rom. xii. 2 ; 1 Cor. i. 20 ; ii. 6, 8 ; iii. 18 ; 2 Cor. iv. 4;
Gal. i. 4 ; Eph. i. 21 ; ii. 2 ; vi. 12 ; 1 Tim. vi. 17 ; 2 Tim. iv. 10 ;
Titus ii. 12.

[2] Acts iii. 19.   [3] Rev. xi. 15.   [4] 1 Cor. xv. 24.
[5] 2 Tim. i. 9 ; and Titus i. 2 : Gr. *πρὸ χρόνων αἰωνίων* : translated,

the well-known words, " Jesus Christ, the same yesterday, to day, and for the ages," first spoken to Hebrews, who were passing out of one " age " into another, imply that through these " ages " a Saviour is needed, and will be found, as much as " yesterday," and " to day," that is in the past and in the present. The " God of ages " lives from age to age, or as our Version translates it " for ever and ever." [1]   " Because He lives, we shall live also." [2]   All things are ours : death or life ; things present or things to come.[3]

Now it will be found that in all the places where this name " El Olam," occurs, there is always a reference, sometimes more hidden, sometimes more open, to the distinct stages of God's dealings with His creatures.   Thus the first occurrence of this name is when Abraham learns that the bondmaid must be cast out, and that the better covenant is with the son of the freewoman.   So Moses, " the man of God," calls upon this name, saying, " From everlasting to everlasting thou art God," only after he has learnt that he himself must pass away, and not enter the promised land, and cries out, " Thou turnest man to destruction : again thou sayest, Return, ye children of men." [4]   So again Isaiah, when he would comfort Israel under the hidings of God's face, asks, " Hast thou not known, that the

---

in our Authorised Version, " before the world began."   The Vulgate translation here is, " Ante sæcularia tempora," which is as literal a rendering as possible.

[1] Rev. xv. 7.

[2] St. John xiv. 19.

[3] Rom. viii. 38.

[4] Psalm xc. 2, 3.

Everlasting God, the Creator of the ends of the earth, fainteth not, neither is weary,"[1] though His work, now as in creation, advances through successive evenings and mornings unto the perfect day. So again Jeremiah, when he calls the LORD the " King of ages," who " hath made the earth by His wisdom, and hath stretched out the heavens by His discretion," speaks at once of His varying operations; now bringing clouds, and now scattering them; at one time "causing the vapours to ascend from the ends of the earth," and at another " bringing forth the wind out of His treasuries."[2] So Micah, foreseeing the days when " many nations shall say, Come and let us go up to the mountain of the Lord," when " they shall beat their swords into ploughshares, and their spears into pruninghooks," speaks of the same name, even of " Him, whose goings forth have been from of old, from everlasting," who " shall now be great unto the ends of the earth."[3] St. Paul speaks yet more clearly of the same name, and of the " revelation of the mystery, which has been kept secret from the age-times, but is now made manifest, according to the commandment of the Everlasting or Age-working God; "[4] and again of the " King of ages," the blessed God, by whose grace the " glorious gospel was committed to his

---

[1] Isa. xl. 28. [2] Jer. x. 10, 12, 13.

[3] Mic. iv. 2; and v. 2, 4.

[4] Rom. xvi. 25, 26: Gr. μυστήριον χρόνοις αἰωνίοις σεσιγημένον . . κατ' ἐπιταγὴν τοῦ αἰωνίου Θεοῦ.

charge," that " Christ Jesus came into the world to
save sinners." [1] And, if I err not, the same title,
" God who liveth for the ages of ages," where it
meets us in the final Revelation, when some are
seen " with harps of gold, standing on the sea of
glass," while others are yet to suffer the " seven last
plagues, for in them is filled up the wrath of God," [2]
assures us of the same truth, that long as the fall
and its bitter fruits remain, with vials of wrath and
judgment through " ages " and " ages of ages," [3] One
lives through all these ages, who is ever the same,
and able to save to the uttermost all that come to God
by Him, seeing He ever liveth to make intercession
for them. [4] Thus every reference to this name is
significant, though few yet know its significance ;
for even to this day the prophet's words are true,
" Verily, Thou art a God that hidest thyself, O God
of Israel, the Saviour." [5]

Such is this name, and it is a witness, how, in
words or names which are often unnoticed, Scripture
may be teaching secrets of God's wise purpose, which
are hidden even from the elect, till the time comes for
their fuller revelation. My assured conviction is that
the deepest things in Scripture, as in our common
daily life,—things which lie at the very foundation
of our being here,—are things which are not and
cannot be openly spoken of to all, while yet they are

---

[1] 1 Tim. i. 14–17 : Gr. βασιλεὺς αἰώνων.

[2] Rev. xv. 1, 2, 7.   [3] Rev. xiv. 4.

[4] Heb. vii. 25.   [5] Isa. xlv. 15.

assumed, and often indirectly alluded to. Certainly
in the Patriarchal lives Divine secrets, which have
taken ages for their revelation, were hidden under apparently unimportant acts or words, which few notice.
God said to Abraham, " In Isaac shall thy seed be
called." "That is," says the Apostle Paul, "they
which are the children of the flesh, these are not the
children of God, but the children of the promise are
counted for the seed."[1]   Again it is written, " Abraham had two sons, the one by a bondmaid, the other
by a freewoman." But in the history of this bondmaid and freewoman, and of their seeds, as the
Apostle shews, we have the secret both of the law
and gospel, and of the passing away of the one, and
the abiding of the other.[2] Just so the name " El
Olam," rarely used, yet always in special connexions,
opens a secret, ignorance of which may keep us unconscious of God's advancing revelation, and leave us,
like the Jew, still clinging to that which is abolished,
when something better has already been revealed.
Blessed are they, who like Abraham and Moses in
the days of old, and like Paul and John when the
Jewish age was vanishing away, have learnt even a
little of this secret of the " ages," for it is " as a light
in a dark place, until the day dawn, and the day-star
arise in our hearts." [3]

---

[1] Rom. ix. 7, 8.   [2] Gal. iv. 22, 30.

[3] 2 Pet. i. 19.

7

LORD OF HOSTS, OR JEHOVAH SABAOTH

THE last name of God which the Old Testament gives us is " Jehovah Sabaoth " or " LORD of Hosts." A special peculiarity attaches to this title, namely, that it is only known in the general failure of God's elect Israel. It is never found in the books of Moses, or in that of Joshua and the Judges, or in Job, or in the Proverbs, or Ecclesiastes. It occurs but rarely in the books of Kings and the Chronicles, and not much oftener in the Psalms. But in most of the Prophets, especially in those who most keenly felt the failure of Israel in the promised land, the name meets us constantly : nearly eighty times in Jeremiah : fourteen in the two short chapters of Haggai : very nearly fifty times in Zechariah, and twenty-five in the brief concluding prophecy of Malachi.

Now this fact itself is significant, shewing that the teaching or lesson which this name conveys belongs to a certain stage in the experience of God's elect people. Speaking generally, every name of God is revealed to meet some felt need of the creature : but some needs are sooner felt than others. All awakened souls feel in some degree that they are needy. The names " Elohim " and " Jehovah," that is God in covenant, yet righteous, may both be known at the very earliest stage and on the lowest platform. We have only to know ourselves as " void and formless," as this earth was when God began His work upon it, and we shall see something at least of the value of His first most blessed name " Elohim." As we learn that man " became a living soul," and is therefore under law, we shall see the riches laid up for us in " Jehovah," who is both righteous, and who gives to man His own righteousness. The higher relationships of God are only known as we advance in the appointed way, some of the most precious being learnt out of our very failure, and even through the judgments which it brings upon us. As we feel our need of His very life to bring forth the seed of promise, we shall know Him as the " Almighty," who gives Himself to us, and makes us partakers of His own fruitfulness. As we see how even Gentiles have a knowledge of God, we shall know Him as the " Most High," who has a priesthood far wider than that which we have first known, that is the priesthood of the election. The name " El Olam," the " God of Ages," is only learnt through a more painful experience. Abraham and Moses did not know it till the one had seen how Hagar must be cast out, and the other that he could not lead Israel into Canaan, but must himself pass

away before God's elect could inherit the land beyond
Jordan. It is so with this last name, " LORD of
Hosts " or " Sabaoth." It is not learnt while we are
bondmen in Egypt, or while we are still in our experience only in the wilderness. It is not even
learnt when we first cross Jordan, and are victorious
in the promised land, that is, when we first apprehend
our place as risen with Christ, and stand upon His
promise, as more than conquerors over wicked spirits
in heavenly places.[1] It is when Israel has failed, not
in Egypt or the desert only, but in the land of
promise, that the name " Jehovah Sabaoth " is first
learnt ; and not until Israel is divided, and in peril
of being led captive out of the land, does it become
the name to which the prophets seem instinctively
to turn for comfort and deliverance. In a word, we
do not know this name, the " LORD of Hosts," till we
have learnt the Church's fall, and that the " hosts of
Israel " [2] can no longer help us, for they are bitterly
divided and destroying one another. But though
Israel fails, God ever remains, and as the " LORD of
Hosts," there is help in Him, very specially when His
elect have no other helper. Therefore, when all things
shake, the Psalmist says, " The LORD of Hosts is with
us, though the earth be removed, and the waters
roar ; and though the mountains be carried into the
midst of the sea." [3] God is and must be ever sufficient,
for a ruined church as for a ruined world. And the

---

[1] Eph. vi. 12.   [2] Numb. i. 52 ; ii. 4, 6, 8, 11, 13, &c.
[3] Psalm xlvi. 3, 7, 11.

Church, because of the deposit committed to her, may need His help even more than the unbelieving world, which is yet so far from Him.

Let us then turn to some of the places where this name occurs, that we may better see its value. We first find it, three or four times, in the earlier chapters of the First Book of Kings, commonly called the First Book of Samuel. Now that book, as indeed every other book of Holy Scripture, has its special aim. Its object is to shew how the failure of the priests in Israel led, first to a prophet taking their place, and then how the failure of the prophet, who made his sons judges, though they walked not in his ways, led to the people asking a king, to go before them and judge them like the nations; [1] in all which, as the LORD then said to Samuel, "They have not rejected thee, but they have rejected me, that I should not reign over them." [2] Henceforward, according to their own wish, they were to be "like the nations," [3] with a king, who "should go before them and fight their battles," and who, to this end, "when he saw any strong or valiant man, took him unto him," thus by strength or gift, instead of in the faith of a present God, to save Israel. [4] For their wish was to have something strong before their eyes, to do those things for them which God Himself had covenanted to do,—

---

[1] In illustration of all this, see " *The Mystery of the Kingdom, traced through the Books of Kings*; " Part i. pp. 44–58.

[2] 1 Sam. viii. 7. [3] 1 Sam. viii. 21.

[4] 1 Sam. xiv. 52.

something or some one who should take His place, as
though the LORD were absent from them. It is in
this state of things, with priests like Hophni and
Phinehas, who " make God's people to transgress,"
and with the ark, now taken by Philistines, and then
left for years in Kirjath-Jearim, that the name of
the " LORD of Hosts, which dwelleth between the
cherubims," first appears in Holy Scripture. As is so
common in the ways of God, it is a sufferer, a barren
woman, who first knows this name and puts her trust
in it.[1] We next find it where the army of Israel is
smitten before the Philistines : [2] then in the mouth
of David, " the stripling," when he meets Goliath of
Gath, " not with sword or shield, but in the name of
the LORD of Hosts, the God of Israel." [3] At this
stage of Israel's history, the name, " Jehovah Sabaoth,"
very rarely meets us. And it is possible that at this
time its true meaning was little understood,—perhaps
even misunderstood,—by those who yet used it. A
soul which deals with God, and listens to His word,
constantly utters truths which are above the speaker's
perfect apprehension ; which therefore, if he attempted
to explain them, might be, not mis-stated only, but
even more or less denied. Peter, for example, when
the Holy Ghost was given, preached that " the
Spirit should be poured out upon all flesh," while yet
he was unprepared to receive this as a truth, when it
came before him practically in the call of the Gentiles

---

[1] 1 Sam. i. 2, 11.   [2] 1 Sam. iv. 2, 4.

[3] 1 Sam. xvii. 45.

in the person of Cornelius.[1] It is possible enough,
therefore, that, when this name, " LORD of Hosts," was
first revealed to God's elect, they may have linked
the title in their thoughts with earthly hosts or
with the hosts of Israel. But the utterances of the
prophets, where this name occurs so often, shew us
its true import, and what it is given to reveal to
God's divided and distressed people.

For in the mouth of the prophets this name has no
uncertain sound. It tells of One, who in the ruin of
His Church on earth, is yet the Lord of heavenly hosts;
who therefore, whatever may be the failure of His
elect on earth, in relation to the dispensation, that is,
to that which is committed to them, can and will yet
perfectly fulfil His purpose of blessing to the world,
perhaps even more fully through the very failure of
His people. With the prophets the " LORD of Hosts "
is the " God of heaven " and of the " hosts of heaven,"
through whom He can fulfil His pleasure, though
men on earth rebel or turn from Him.[2] So Isaiah,
in the days of Ahaz, " who walked after the abominations of the heathen," until Judah was smitten and

---

[1] Acts ii. 17 ; and x. 14, 28.

[2] I may note here that Daniel is one of the very few prophets
who do not use the title " LORD of Hosts," but has instead the
name, the " God of heaven." (e.g. Dan. ii. 18, 28, 37 ; iv. 37 ;
v. 23.) We find the same name in the decree of Cyrus ; (2 Chron.
xxxvi. 23 ; and Ezra i. 2 ;) and in the prayer of Nehemiah.
(Neh. i. 4, 5 ; and ii. 4, 20.) It seems as if the two titles were
substantially equivalent. Compare Psalm cxlviii. 1, 2. We find
the expression, " Host of heaven," in 1 Kings xxii. 19 ; 2 Chron.
xviii. 18 ; &c.

led captive,[1] so that " the daughter of Zion was left
as a cottage in a vineyard, as a lodge in a garden of
cucumbers, and as a besieged city," turns to this
name for succour, saying, " Except the LORD of Hosts
had left unto us a very small remnant, we should
have been as Sodom, and we should have been like
unto Gomorrah." [2] So again, " in the year that King
Uzziah died,"—who had freed the people from the
Philistines, and to whom the Ammonites had given
gifts, " for he had built towers in Jerusalem, and had
a host of fighting men, so that his name was spread
far abroad," [3]—the vision which Isaiah saw was of a
Lord stronger than the earthly king who had passed
away,—a Lord " whose train filled the temple," and
still " cried, Holy, Holy, Holy, LORD of Hosts: the
whole earth is full of His glory." [4] So again, when
the Kings of Israel and Syria were confederate
against Judah, and " the heart of the people was
moved as the trees of the wood are moved with the
wind," the LORD thus spake, saying, " Say not, A
confederacy, neither fear ye their fear, nor be afraid ;
but sanctify the LORD of Hosts Himself, and let
Him be your fear ; and He shall be for a sanctuary.
. . . the zeal of the LORD of Hosts will perform
this." [5] It is so always. It is the " LORD of Hosts "
who punishes His people for their unfaithfulness.[6]
It is again the " LORD of Hosts," who, when they

---

[1] 2 Chron. xxviii. 1–5.

[2] Isa. i. 8, 9.

[3] 2 Chron. xxvi. 6–15.

[4] Isa. vi. 1–3.

[5] Isa. vii. 2 ; viii. 11–14; ix. 7.

[6] Isa. ix. 13, 19.

have been chastened, smites their adversary and brings them help and full deliverance. " Therefore thus saith the LORD of Hosts, O my people, be not afraid of the Assyrian : he shall smite thee with a rod, and shall lift up his staff against thee : but yet a very little while and the indignation shall cease, and the LORD of Hosts shall stir up a scourge for him, and his burden shall be taken from thy shoulder."[1] " Like as a lion roaring on his prey, so shall the LORD of Hosts come down to fight for Mount Zion, and for the hill thereof: as birds flying, so will the LORD of Hosts defend Jerusalem : defending also He will deliver it." [2]

And it is very especially when His people are captive, and have no might to help themselves, that this name is most often repeated by the prophets for their comfort. As I have already said, Jeremiah in the destruction of Jerusalem uses it nearly eighty times, and Haggai constantly repeats it in his exhortations to the little remnant, who have gone up out of Babylon to build again the house of the LORD :—
" Yet now be strong, O Zerubbabel, and be strong, O Joshua, son of Josedech, and be strong, all ye people of the land, and work ; for I am with you, saith the LORD of Hosts. For thus saith the LORD of Hosts, Yet once, it is a little while, and I will shake the heavens, and the earth, and the sea ; and I will fill this house with glory, saith the LORD of Hosts. The silver is mine, and the gold is mine,

---

[1] Isa. x. 12, 24–27.   [2] Isa. xxxi. 4, 5.

saith the LORD of Hosts. The glory of this latter
house shall be greater than the former, saith the
LORD of Hosts; and in this place will I give peace,
saith the LORD of Hosts. . . . For I have chosen
thee, saith the LORD of Hosts." [1] With the last of
the old prophets it is the same. He pours out his
complaint at the growing corruption :— "They that
work wickedness are set up; yea, they that tempt
God are even delivered." But a little remnant yet
" fear Him, and think upon His name." "And they
shall be mine, saith the LORD of Hosts, in the day
when I make up my jewels, and I will spare them as
a man spareth his own son that serveth him." [2] Thus
must He ever answer the cry, "O LORD, God, of
Hosts, how long wilt thou be angry against the
prayer of thy people? Turn us again, O LORD, God,
of Hosts, cause thy face to shine, and we shall be
saved." [3]

And Scripture is full of illustrations of the way
in which the "LORD of Hosts" uses His hosts for the
correction and deliverance of His people, and for the
punishment of His adversaries, with terrible displays
of just judgment. David is an example. All Israel
have accepted him as king :— "The LORD had given
him rest round about from all his enemies." Then
comes the temptation to number the people, and to
count how strong he is. "And Joab gave the number
of the people unto David ; all they of Israel were

---

[1] Haggai ii. 4–9, 23. [2] Mal. iii. 16, 17.

[3] Psalm lxxx. 4, 19.

eight hundred thousand valiant men that drew the sword, and the men of Judah were five hundred thousand men." Can these mighty men of valour help, if God is forgotten ? Was not David stronger, unaided and alone, when he replied to the taunt of Goliath of Gath by " the name of the LORD of Hosts," than he now is with a thousand thousand valiant men ? The LORD'S answer to the numbering of the people is to shew His host. " God sent an angel, the angel of the LORD, destroying throughout the coasts of Israel. And David lifted up his eyes, and saw the angel of the LORD, standing between earth and heaven, having a drawn sword in his hand stretched out over Jerusalem ; and there fell of Israel seventy thousand men, for the LORD sent a pestilence upon Israel." [1] So again when Ahab gathers his host to go against Ramoth-gilead, and the King of Judah joins him, saying, " I am as thou art, my people as thy people, my horses as thy horses," the prophet of the LORD sees another host :—" And Micaiah said, I saw the LORD sitting on His throne, and all the host of heaven standing by Him, on His right hand and on His left." And of this host " a spirit went forth," and, spite of all the hosts of Israel, by this spirit Ahab is deceived and drawn to his destruction. We read, " A certain man drew a bow at a venture, and smote the King of Israel between the joints of his harness." [2] A chance shot, as men speak,—was it not rather an angel of the LORD ?—silently accom-

---

[1] 1 Chron. xxi. 2-16.   [2] 1 Kings xxii. 19-22, 34.

plishes the threatened judgment. So again, in the case of Elisha, when " the King of Syria sent horses and chariots, and a great host, to take him, and they came by night and compassed the city round about. And the servant of the man of God said unto his master, Alas, my master, how shall we do? And he answered, Fear not; for they that be with us are more than they that be with them. And Elisha prayed, and said, LORD, I pray thee, open his eyes that he may see. And the LORD opened the eyes of the young man; and he saw, and, behold, the mountain was full of horses and chariots of fire round about Elisha." By them the prophet is delivered. " And the bands of Syria came no more into the land of Israel." [1] So again, when the King of Assyria sent Rabshakeh with a great host against Jerusalem, and Hezekiah, who had no power to save his people, cries for help to " Him who dwelleth between the cherubim," the answer is this:—" Thus saith the LORD concerning the King of Assyria, He shall not come into this city, nor shoot an arrow there. By the way that he came, by the same shall he return; for I will defend this city to save it for mine own sake, and for my servant David's sake. . . . The zeal of the LORD of Hosts shall do this. And it came to pass that night, that the angel of the LORD went out, and smote in the camp of the Assyrians a hundred fourscore and five thousand; and when they arose in the morning, behold, they were all dead corpses." [2] Well might

---

[1] 2 Kings vi. 11–18.   [2] 2 Kings xviii. 17; xix. 21–33.

the Psalmist cry, " O LORD of Hosts, who is a strong LORD, like unto thee, or to thy faithfulness round about thee ? Thou rulest the raging of the sea : when the waves thereof arise, thou stillest them." [1]

And it had been ever thus, though in earlier days God's people knew it less clearly : for love makes provision for the helpless babe, even while it is all unconscious of the service rendered to it. God's hosts had always been serving His elect. Lot leaves Abram, and having first pitched his tent toward Sodom, soon dwells there and is seen sitting in the gate.[2] Now the judgment of Sodom was at the very doors. " And there came two angels to Sodom, and Lot seeing them rose up to meet them. And they said, Hast thou any here ? Bring them out, for we will destroy this place, because the cry of them is waxen great before the face of the LORD, and the LORD hath sent us to destroy it. And when the morning arose, then the angels hastened Lot, and laid hold upon his hand, and upon the hand of his wife, and upon the hand of his two daughters ; the LORD being merciful to him ; and they brought them forth without the city." [3] So again, when Hagar flies from Abram's house, the " angel of the LORD found her in the wilderness."[4] So too with Jacob, when an exile from his home he lighted upon a certain place, and lay down to sleep with a stone for his pillow. But help is near him ; for he sees " a ladder

---

[1] Psalm lxxxix. 8, 9. [2] Gen. xiii. 12 ; xiv. 12 ; xix. 1.
[3] Gen. xix. 1-17. [4] Gen. xvi. 7-11.

set upon the earth, the top of which reached even
to heaven, and behold, angels of God ascended and
descended on it." [1]   So again, when he went on his
way, " the angels of God met him; and when he saw
them, he said, This is God's host." [2]   It is so always,
where there is real need.   " The angel of the LORD
encampeth round about them that fear Him, and
delivereth them." [3]

But it is the New Testament which especially
opens this ministry of the heavenly host to God's
elect.   They constantly appear, wherever there is
need to be supplied or danger to be averted.   " The
angel of the Lord appeared to Joseph," [4] and to
Zechariah, [5] and to Mary, [6] and to the shepherds, [7]
when " there was with the angel a multitude of the
heavenly host, praising God, and saying, Glory to
God in the highest, and on earth peace, goodwill toward men ; " in every instance commencing their
message with the words, " Fear not ; " for the opening of the spirit-world, even if it is to bring us help,
ever more or less awakens the sense of the weakness
of flesh and blood, and that in our present state we
are little fit to deal directly with heavenly realities.
Yet these heavenly hosts ever wait upon us.   " Are
they not all ministering spirits, sent forth to minister
for them who shall be heirs of salvation ? " [8]   Their
ceaseless ministry to our Lord is the pattern of their

---

[1] Gen. xxviii. 12.
[2] Gen. xxxii. 1, 2.
[3] Psalm xxxiv. 7.
[4] St. Matt. i. 20.
[5] St. Luke i. 13, 19.
[6] St. Luke i. 26, 30.
[7] St. Luke ii. 9, 10, 13.
[8] Heb. i. 14.

ministry to us, for " we are members of His body, of His flesh, and of His bones." [1] How they were ever serving Him unseen, the Gospels shew. We have seen how angels sang at His birth : angels no less were near to guide His early steps, first to Egypt, and then again into the land of Israel : [2] angels came and ministered to Him after His temptation : [3] an angel strengthened Him in the garden : [4] angels at His grave rolled away the stone, and declared to His weeping disciples, that " He is not here, but risen." [5] And that He was conscious of this ministry, and taught His disciples to expect it, His repeated words declare :—" Thinkest thou that I cannot now pray to my Father, and He shall presently give me more than twelve legions of angels ? " [6] " Verily, verily, henceforward ye shall see heaven open, and the angels of God ascending and descending upon the Son of Man." [7]

The Apostles' lives are full of illustrations of this heavenly service. Peter in prison, [8] Philip guided into the desert, [9] Paul in the storm, [10] John in Patmos, [11] all are witnesses of the angelic help which is ever waiting upon the Lord's servants. To John especially it was given, not only to " hear the voice of many angels round about the throne," [12] but also to see how to these angels is committed not a little of

---

[1] Eph. v. 30. 　　　　　　 [2] St. Matt. ii. 13, 19.
[3] St. Matt. iv. 11. 　　　　 [4] St. Luke xxii. 43.
[5] St. Matt. xxviii. 2, 6. 　　 [6] St. Matt. xxvi. 53.
[7] St. John i. 51. 　 [8] Acts xii. 8. 　 [9] Acts viii. 26.
[10] Acts xxvii. 23. 　 [11] Rev. i. 1. 　 [12] Rev. v. 11.

the government of this world. " Not unto angels, but
to man, hath God put in subjection the world to
come ; " [1] but " the things that are," as seen by John,
are in the hands of heavenly hosts, whose work it is
to fulfil God's will, both in the world, and towards
His people.   Not only are there " angels of the
Churches," [2] and " angels round about the throne," [3]
but there are " angels standing on the four corners of
the earth, holding the four winds of the earth, that
the wind should not blow upon the earth, nor on
the sea, nor on any tree ; " [4] there are " angels with
trumpets," the sounding of which is followed by
judgments upon the earth, and sea, and the foun-
tains of waters ; [5] there are " angels with vials, in
which is filled up the wrath of God ; " [6] there are
" angels bound in the great river Euphrates," who
are " prepared to slay the third part of men ; " [7]
there is an " angel of the waters," who says, " Thou
art righteous, O Lord, for thou hast judged thus ; " [8]
there is an " angel standing in the sun," who declares the judgment of " all flesh ; " [9] there is an
" angel with the seal of the living God," whose work
it is " to seal the servants of God upon their foreheads ; " [10] there is an " angel, flying through heaven,
with the everlasting Gospel, to preach to them that

---

[1] Heb. ii. 5, 6.

[2] Rev. i. 20 ; iii. 1, 8, 12, 18, &c.

[3] Rev. vii. 11.   [4] Rev. vii. 1.

[5] Rev. viii. 6–12.   [6] Rev. xv. 1, 7.

[7] Rev. ix. 14, 15.   [8] Rev. xvi. 5.

[9] Rev. xix. 17, 18.   [10] Rev. vii. 2, 3.

dwell upon the earth, and to every nation, and
kindred, and tongue, and people;"¹ there is an
"angel who cries, Babylon is fallen, is fallen, that
great city, because she made all nations drink of the
wine of the wrath of her fornication;"² and, to
speak of but one other, though there are many,
there is an "angel which says, Come hither, I will
shew thee the Bride, the Lamb's wife," and who,
when John falls down to worship him, says, "See
thou do it not, for I am thy fellow servant; worship
God."³ From first to last the Revelation is full of
angels, who are "sent" by Him who is their Lord,
"to testify these things unto His servants for the
Churches."⁴

There may be a stage when we are hardly fit to
see these things. Even when seen, as in the case of
the beloved John, the vision may be so bright that
for a moment the seer falls down before a fellow-
servant, as Cornelius "fell down and worshipped
Peter," who "took him up, saying, Stand up, I myself also am a man."⁵ Yet such a vision never is
forgotten. The seer learns from it, in a way above
all words, that "the light affliction, which is but for
a moment, is not worthy to be compared to the glory
which shall be revealed in us."⁶ Even the faith that
there are such hosts of ministering spirits cannot

---

¹ Rev. xiv. 6.   ² Rev. xiv. 8.
³ Rev. xxi. 9.
⁴ Rev. xxii. 16. Gr. μαρτυρῆσαι ὑμῖν ταῦτα ἐπὶ ταῖς ἐκκλησίαις.
⁵ Acts x. 25, 26.   ⁶ Rom. viii. 18.

but comfort the oppressed. Therefore the Apostle James, regarding the "labourers who have reaped the fields, and whose hire is kept back by fraud," by " rich men who shall weep and howl for the miseries which are coming on them," simply says, "The cries of them which have reaped are entered into the ears of the Lord of Sabaoth."[1] They shall be righted, if not by man, yet by the "Lord of Hosts." All are called to know how near He is, and how near are His unseen hosts, who do His pleasure. For, as the Apostle says, "Ye are not come unto a mount that may be touched, and to the sound of a trumpet, and to the voice of words. . . . But ye are come unto Mount Sion, to the city of the living God, the heavenly Jerusalem, and to an innumerable company of angels, to the general assembly and church of the firstborn, which are written in heaven, and to God, the Judge of all, and to the spirits of just men made perfect."[2] This name, the "Lord of Hosts," reveals it all, that we may know what help is ever near, in Him who "gives His angels charge concerning us, to keep us in all our ways."[3]

It may perhaps be said, that, though such things were known by saints of old, Christians have little or no experience of them now. But surely it is not so. There are few among the truly believing poor, who have not facts to speak of, which prove that angel help is still as near as ever. If men have not proved

---

[1] St. James v. 4.   [2] Heb. xii. 18, 23.

[3] Psalm xci. 11.

it, is it not because they have not needed such help, or have not confidently looked for it from the living God? Thanks be to God, not a few yet know that the " LORD of Hosts is with us." Such can only bless Him for the trials through which they have learnt this name, and can therefore say, not with their lips only, but from their heart, " Holy, Holy, Holy, Lord, God, of Sabaoth, heaven and earth are full of the majesty of thy glory."

8

FATHER, SON, AND HOLY GHOST

THE names of God which we have so far considered
all belong to the Old Covenant, under which "that
which may be known of God" was taught "here a
little and there a little,"[1] to suit the state in which
men were, not knowing God as He has since revealed
Himself in Christ, and by His Spirit. The perfect
name is declared to us by Jesus Christ, our Lord,
even "the name of the Father, and of the Son, and
of the Holy Ghost;" in which is united and summed
up all that was taught of old in the names revealed
to patriarchs and prophets under the Old Covenant.
Here, as much as in the patriarchal lives, or in the
shadows of the law, Augustine's well-known words
hold good, that "the New Testament lies hid in the
Old, while the Old is opened in the New."[2] The
"name of the Father, and of the Son, and of the Holy
Ghost," only opens in its fulness what was taught in
part, and under a veil, in the names "Elohim,"
"Jehovah," "El Shaddai," and "Adonai."

This New Testament name comes to us from the

---

[1] Isa. xxviii. 10.
[2] Augustine : *Quæst. in Exod.* § 73, (on chapter xx. 19.)

mouth of the risen Christ, and is yet revealed by Him to those, who, having known Him after the flesh, and in His divided and partial manifestations, have come, through the knowledge of His cross and resurrection, to receive a mission from Him, to " go and teach all nations, baptizing them into the name of the Father, and of the Son, and of the Holy Ghost." [1]   For He is still amongst us, and by His Spirit can yet " make known His name," [2] that " our hearts being comforted and knit together in love," we may come in due time " unto all riches of the full assurance of understanding, to the acknowledgment of the mystery of God, even of the Father, and of Christ." [3]   His will is that we should know Him, and that we are partakers of His very nature, [4] thus called to reveal, not in word only, but in deed and life, something of that glory which is set before us in this last most wondrous name, of " the Father, and of the Son, and of the Holy Ghost."

Let us then turn to this name, and may our Lord Himself declare it to us, that the love wherewith the Father has loved Him may be in us, and He in us. [5]

First then " the name of the Father, and of the Son, and of the Holy Ghost," is one name, not three or many. [6]   Our Lord did not say, " Baptizing them into the names," but " into the name, of the Father,

---

[1] St. Matt. xxviii. 19.   [2] St. John xvii. 6.   [3] Col. ii. 2.

[4] 2 St. Peter i. 4.   [5] St. John xvii. 26.

[6] See the passages from St. Jerome and Euthymius, quoted by Cornelius a Lapide, on St. Matt. xxviii. 19.

and of the Son, and of the Holy Ghost." For, as He said to the Scribe, "The Lord our God is one Lord." [1] What this name therefore declares is One God, in what, for want of a better word, we call Three Persons ; a " Father," who eternally produces Himself in His " Son," and by His " Spirit," and who, in His very being, even as in His works, is a witness of unity in plurality, and of a giving forth out of Himself, and a communion with Himself, which to our fallen senses seems well-nigh impossible. We shall see what is involved in this Threefold Name as we look more closely into it. Here I only notice that it is " the Name," not " Names," of " the Father, the Son, and the Holy Ghost."

Now this truth, of a diversity in the unity of God, is no new truth. It has been assumed, and more or less expressed, in the varied names of God which were declared under the older revelation. We saw how in " Elohim," who said, " Let us make man in our image, after our likeness," and again " The man is become as one of us," [2] there was, to say the least, some intimation of plurality ; while in the fact that the same name, " Elohim," which is plural, is joined with singular adjectives and verbs, and that He who calls Himself " Elohim " says of Himself distinctly, " There is no God beside me," [3] we have still more direct assertion of His unity. In the contrast too between the import of the names " Elohim," who is in a covenant-relationship which never fails, and

[1] St. Mark xii. 29.　　[2] Gen. i. 26 ; iii. 22.　　[3] Isa. xlv. 5.

" Jehovah," who loves in virtue of quality and must judge evil, and yet makes His creatures righteous by giving them His own righteousness, and no less in the names " El Elyon," the " Most High," from whom we all proceed, and " El Shaddai," the " Pourer-forth," who gives forth from Himself His life and Spirit to His servants, there were repeated suggestions of that unutterable fulness of Love, and Wisdom, and Power, which are so wondrously expressed in " the Name of the Father, the Son, and the Holy Ghost." I may say more. For it is not Holy Scripture only which bears this witness. In our very nature, which shews that fatherhood, sonship, and the spirit of both, are in every man, we have intimations of the mystery of Father, Son, and Spirit, in God, unless we are prepared to grant that the creature can possess and be more than the Creator. It is true that in man, in his fallen state, personality seems to be that which cuts off one man from another. Yet even here we are in one another. Even since the fall the mystery of love answers every objection to the apparent difficulty how two can be one, and one even in a third; for love ever draws two to be one, and by their mingled being forms a third, who has been in both, and proceeds from both, and in whom, in another form, the two are yet one. Still more surely do we know, for Scripture asserts it, that the woman, and therefore her seed in her, was in the man as formed in God's image, until that deep sleep fell upon Adam, in which he lost his primal form, and that which

hitherto had been united and one became divided.[1]
This is a great mystery. Yet in it we may see how
the unity, and yet the plurality also, of God are revealed in man created in His image. It is one of the
many preludings which both Nature and Scripture
give us of that great harmony, which is perfectly expressed in the Name of " the Father, the Son, and the
Holy Ghost."

I can barely touch this here, but I note it in
passing; for the doctrine of the Trinity, that is of
what God is, as " Father, Son, and Holy Ghost," has
too often been regarded, even by believers, as an
isolated truth, standing apart from, and having no
relation to, our human hearts and human consciousness; whereas, inasmuch as man was made in God's
image, what God is in Himself is the very ground,
not only of our relation to Him, but of our very
being, and of our true knowledge of ourselves and of
our duties. If God is love, and love requires (for to
dwell in solitude is not love) such a communion and
relationship as is expressed in " the Name of the
Father, the Son, and the Holy Ghost," then our true
life, if we are His sons, must have the same characteristics, and be a life of communion and relationship. On the other hand, the very cravings of our
nature for communion and relationship witness, that
in Him, " in whom we live, and move, and have our
being," [2] there must be the substance of that, of which
our life, with its relationships and communions, is but

---

[1] Gen. ii. 23.   [2] Acts xvii. 28.

the shadow. This is what our Lord reveals, in making known to His disciples " the Name of the Father, the Son, and the Holy Ghost." And just in proportion as we really know that God is " Father, Son, and Holy Ghost," we shall reflect something of the fellowship and love, which such a name declares to us. The world's selfishness is the result of not knowing what He truly is, from whom we come, and for whom we were created.[1]

What then does this name declare? It says that God is Father,—that therefore there must be a Son,—and that the Father and the Son are One in One Spirit. Thus it speaks of a life which brings forth life,—of a life which is brought forth,—and of a still further proceeding forth of life, which nevertheless is all one. Who is sufficient for these things ; for life is that which everywhere eludes our grasp. And yet our Lord Himself reveals this to us, for as we see it we reflect and are transformed into the same image.

First, God is " The Father." In Himself, as God, there is this relationship with One, who, though He is " with God," and also " is God," is no less " His Only-begotten Son." [2] Fatherhood is not confined to creatures. Rather creatures are and can be fathers, because in the Divine Nature there is both a Father and a Son. What this relation expresses of an eternal love between Him who begets and Him who is begotten,—what it tells us of a union and communion in Him who is the source and ground

---

[1] Col. i. 16.　　　　　[2] St. John i. 1, 14, 18.

of all being,—in its height and depth transcends all
language. Yet we have a broken shadow of it in
every earthly father, and in all fatherhood, even
as seen in this world, where sin is still working.
" Father " tells us of a source of life ; of one in whom
his sons have been,[1] and from whom they come, and
whose image and likeness they are called to manifest.
" Father " tells us of relationship, in nature and in
blood ; and of a love, which, because it is in virtue of
relationship, must be unchanging and unchanged,
even though the son becomes a prodigal ; which
therefore loves him, even when far off, and will fall
on his neck and kiss him, while the rags of the
far country still cover him.[2] " Father " says much
more. It speaks of one who will guide and bear
with babes, " who are borne by him from the belly,
and are carried from the womb ; "[3] it declares that
he who bears this name must educate and rule, and
" as a father charge his sons ; "[4] that he must correct
them also, " for what son is he whom the father
chasteneth not ? "[5] What shall I say more ? " A
father pitieth his children."[6] A father " knoweth
what things his children have need of, before they
ask him."[7] " If a son ask bread of any that is a
father, will the father give him a stone ; or if he ask
a fish, will he give him a serpent ? "[8] Is it not a
father's joy " to lay up for the children, and not the

---

[1] Heb. vii. 10.
[2] St. Luke xv. 12–24.
[3] Isa. xlvi. 3, 4.
[4] 1 Thess. v. 11, 12.
[5] Heb. xii. 7.
[6] Psalm ciii. 13.
[7] St. Luke xii. 30.
[8] St. Luke xi. 11, 13.

children for the fathers ? " [1]   Even if they perish
in some crime, must not a father cry, like David,
" Would God I had died for thee, my son, my son " ? [2]
What then must be the relationship in God, who
is perfect love, between the Father and the Son ?
What must He be, who is " The Father," " of whom
all fatherhood in heaven and earth is named " ? [3]
What must be His love to His beloved Son ? [4]
What must be His will towards all, who in and by
His Son are made His sons, and have come from,
or been begotten by, Him ?

For,—and I would call attention to this,—it is a
Will that is specially declared in all these acts,
which I have referred to as characteristic of a father.
Whether it be the love which begets, or which
guards the babes, or which righteously corrects evil,
even in the sons, or which answers the children's
cry, or which lays up good things for them unasked,
or which, having loved them, loves them to the end,
—every act is the expression of a Will.   " The
Father " is the Will, in the mystery of the ever-
blessed Trinity.   As we look further into the name,
we shall see that it contains more than a Will.
But an eternal Will is the foundation, a Will
which loves and cannot but love, and which shews
itself in Him who comes forth from the Father,
to tell us what the Father is, and to reveal Him
to His creatures.

[1] 2 Cor. xii. 14.   [2] 2 Sam. xviii. 33.
[3] Eph. iii. 15.   [4] St. Matt. iii. 17 ; xvii. 5.

For the name is not " Father " only, but " The Son," who " being the brightness of God's glory, and the express image of His person," [1] reveals the Father and His love, by His works in all creation ; " for by Him were all things created that are in heaven and that are in earth, visible and invisible," [2] to tell out God's glory ; [3] and who, when through our fall we could see no love in such wondrous works, " came forth from the Father, and came into the world," [4] that He might declare His Father's name and nature to us.   Thus, as the Apostle tells us, He is " the Word," who was " with God and was God ; " [5] the " Only-begotten Son, who is in the bosom of the Father, and who hath declared Him ; " [6] " the Light which shineth in the darkness, though the darkness comprehends it not : the true Light which lighteth every man that cometh into the world ; " [7] who says, " I will declare thy name unto my brethren ; " [8] " I will shew you plainly of the Father." [9]   This is He who reveals the Father, and who being Himself " the Son," and thus in personal relation with a Father, not only reveals God, as " the Word," but, by His indwelling in us, makes us as persons sons together with Him.   For to " as many as receive Him He gives power to become the sons of God, even to them which believe in His name, who are born,

---

[1] Heb. i. 3 ; Col. i. 15.
[2] Col. i. 16.
[3] Psalm xix. 1.
[4] St. John xvi. 28.
[5] St. John i. 1.
[6] St. John i. 18.
[7] St. John i. 5, 9. . [8] Heb. ii. 12.
[9] St. John xvi. 25.

not of blood,[1] nor of the will of the flesh, nor of the
will of man, but of God." [2] So, in the wondrous
prayer recorded by St. John, He says, " I have
manifested thy name to the men thou gavest me out
of the world; for the words which thou gavest me
I have given them; and I have declared unto them
thy name and will declare it, that the love wherewith
thou hast loved me may be in them and I in them." [3]

Oh, what a revelation of the Father it is which
the Son has made to men. What a Word has He
been, and is, and ever will be. And what a Will in
the Eternal Father has He revealed to us. Surely
the heavens and earth have told us much, declaring
His glory and shewing His handy work.[4] Sunshine
and rain and fruitful seasons, filling men's hearts
with food and gladness,[5] have said with no uncertain
voice that God loves all and cares for all, seeing that
He is a Giver,[6] even when they know Him not.
But the " Son " has shewn us more, even that death
and pain, which sin has brought, shall be overcome,
and even now may be overcome, in as many as receive
Him, because He Himself, the Lord of all, has stooped
to meet us, and has even come under our curse, and
Himself been made sin for us, though He knew no
sin, that so He might abolish death, and be the

---

[1] Observe the Greek here, ἐξ αἱμάτων, that is " of bloods," re-
ferring to the division caused by the fall. Compare ἐξ ἑνὸς αἵματος,
in Acts xvii. 26–28, where the life is referred to, which we receive
as God's offspring.   [2] St. John i. 10, 13.

[3] St. John xvii. 6, 8, 26.   [4] Psalm xix. 1.

[5] Acts xiv. 17.   [6] Acts xvii. 24.

Creator of a new creation, where sin and death shall
be no more. The Gospels tell it all—how He has revealed the Father to us. For His works are the works
of God. "The Son does nothing of Himself, but what
He seeth the Father do, these things also doeth the
Son in like manner."[1] Are there leprous creatures,
cut off from men, and crying, "Unclean, unclean"?
The Son reveals the Father's Will, and makes them
clean.[2] Are there palsied souls, grievously tormented,
who can do no work for God or man? He speaks,
and the palsied are restored and healed the self-same
hour.[3] Are there others, like Peter's wife's mother,
in whom sin works as a fever, which keeps them in
burning restlessness and disquietude? He yet takes
such by the hand, and the fever leaves them.[4] Are
there others suffering even worse, possessed with
devils, who answer for the possessed, as if they
were himself, and cry, "My name is Legion"? The
"Son" can cast them out.[5] There is no evil He cannot
meet. Bodily or spiritual lameness, blindness, dumb-
ness, deafness, dropsy,[6] a spirit of infirmity, which
bows souls down through long and weary years,[7]—
even death, when the dead are, not only dead "in
the house,"[8] but "laid in the grave," and even
"stinking,"[9]—all yield to Him who is the "Son,"
who thus reveals the "Father." And no less does He

---

[1] St. John v. 19.   [2] St. Matt. viii. 3.   [3] St. Matt. viii. 6, 13.
[4] St. Matt. viii. 14, 15.   [5] St. Mark v. 2–15.
[6] St. Matt. xi. 5 ; St. Luke xiv. 2.   [7] St. Luke xiii. 11.
[8] St. Mark v. 39, 40.   [9] St. John xi. 38, 39.

reveal Him in His terrible rebukes to those, who
"trust in themselves that they are righteous," and
"thank God that they are not as other men;" who
judge of their state God-ward, not by their love, that
is their likeness to their Lord, but by their privileges,
that they are here "clothed with the purple and fine
raiment" of the kingdom, while yet they have no
pity for the lost, who are "full of sores," even "at their
gates," and to whom the very "dogs" shew more
kindness.[1] Who has ever spoken like "The Son" to
judge hypocrisy and wrong? Who has so stripped
deceivers bare, spite of all their outward religious-
ness? Oh blessed yet awful revelation of the Father
through the Son. "He that hath seen Him hath
seen the Father."[2] For "the Word was made flesh,
and dwelt among us, and we beheld His glory, the
glory as of the Only-begotten of the Father, full of
grace and truth."[3]

But "the name" revealed by the risen Lord, and
into which we are baptized, goes even further. For
it is not only the name of the "Father" and of the
"Son," but also of the "Holy Ghost." Now this
word "Ghost" or "Spirit," elsewhere translated
"Breath" or "Wind,"[4] expresses a power unseen but
felt, like the breath of heaven which moves the forest
and the sea;[5] which may come sometimes like a

---

[1] St. Matt. xxiii. 13, 29; St. Luke xvi. 19; xviii. 9, 11.
[2] St. John xiv. 9.   [3] St. John i. 18.
[4] See Job xxxiii. 4; Ezek. xxxvii. 5, 6, 8, &c.; St. John iii. 8.
[5] Isa. vii. 2; Psalm cvii. 25, &c.

strong wind which rends the mountains,[1] or at others as the balmy breath which makes the waters flow ;[2] now blowing on the gardens, that their spices may flow out ;[3] and again breathing upon the sick and dead, that they may live ;[4] always free as the air we breathe, encompassing us about, and even entering into us, as the very breath of life to all creatures. Such is the " Holy Ghost," the very Breath or Spirit of the living God, the worker of the Father's Will. For as at creation He moved upon the waters :[5] as He strove with the old world, when the wickedness of man was great upon the earth :[6] as He came upon judges, prophets, and kings,[7] out of weakness to make them strong, to carry out God's purposes towards His people ; so He yet fulfils God's will in men, now convincing the world of sin, now taking of the things of Christ to shew them to disciples ;[8] giving to one the word of wisdom, to another the word of knowledge, to another gifts of healing, to another divers kinds of tongues ; all being the working of that one and self-same Spirit, who divideth to every man severally as He will.[9] Under this name therefore we get the revelation, not only of a Will and Word in God, but of a Power also, which is indeed Almighty ; a revelation of all, and even more than all, that the

---

[1] 1 Kings xix. 11.
[2] Psalm cxlvii. 18.
[3] Cant. iv. 16.
[4] Ezek. xxxvii. 9.
[5] Gen. i. 2.
[6] Gen. vi. 3.
[7] Judges vi. 34 ; xiv. 6 ; xv. 14 ; 1 Sam. xvi. 13 ; Ezek. iii. 12, 14 ; and xi. 1, 24.
[8] St. John xvi. 8–14.
[9] 1 Cor. xii. 6, 11.

name " El Shaddai " taught of old; for the name
now taught is " Holy Ghost," not power only, but
holy power, even the power of love, which never fails,
until by the sacrifice of itself it has made others
partakers of the same Spirit. Such a Spirit, the
" Spirit " of the " Father " and of the " Son," lifts those
who receive it into a sphere, where the inequalities of
this life are swallowed up in a " communion," " where
there is neither Jew nor Greek, nor bond nor free ; " [1]
where, inspired by God's own Spirit, of holiness and
love, we too may minister His Spirit, and, like His
Son, be not only " living souls," but " quickening
spirits " also,[2] to reveal Him in a world that knows
Him not.

This then is the crowning name, " Father, Son,
and Holy Ghost," the witness that there is in God
all, and more than all, that the creature can need
for its salvation,—a Will in the " Father," who can
never change, to bless and do us good,—a Word in
the " Son," who is no less changeless, to make us know
the Father,—and a Power in the " Holy Ghost," who
is Almighty, to fulfil the Will and Word of God, until
through judgment all things are made new. In the
name, " the Father," we have that love which our
inmost souls require : in the name of " the Son,"
the revelation of that righteousness and truth, which
we no less need to save us from our adversary : in
the name of " the Holy Spirit," the might and power
to conform us to God's will, and to enable us, not

---

[1] Gal. iii. 28.   [2] 1 Cor. xv. 45.

only to enlighten, but to comfort and strengthen, others. And we need the name in all its fulness, " Father, Son, and Holy Ghost." We cannot take one part of it and deny the rest, without robbing God of His glory, and ourselves of the grace which He possesses for us. Have we not seen how some who say that there cannot be a Son in God, while they profess to contend the loudest for His Fatherhood, have come to deny also that He has made any sacrifice for men? They call Him Love, but would take from Him that which is love's inmost impulse, even to give forth one's life to beget another, or to sacrifice what is most precious to us for another. So again the denial of the Godhead of the Son would make the Spirit which He gives us only a creature, which, however helpful, can never make men sons of God, or restore in man God's marred image. Therefore the Church has so earnestly contended for this name, " Father, Son, and Holy Ghost," seeing in it the foundation of all our hopes and aspirations. The more it opens, the more it shews us of the fulness of our God. Oh the depth of the riches here revealed! " Lo, these are parts of His ways, but how little a portion is heard of Him." [1]

Such is this name, which sums up " that which may be known of God," [2] revealed by Christ Himself, to those, who, having first known Him after the flesh, have come in due time, through following Him to His cross, to see and know Him in resurrection also.

Job xxvi. 14.   [2] Rom. i. 19.

Only such souls ever really enter into the fulness here opened to us. Thank God, the fact, that God is what He is, does not depend upon our understanding of it : God does not change, because we cannot see His glory. But the joy and strength of His disciples depends not a little on what they know of Him, and that there is a " Son " in God, who has shewn us the " Father," and given us His " Spirit," so that we too, as sons of God, may " shew forth His virtues." [1] To others the Threefold Name cannot but for awhile be more or less " dark with excess of light," though, because it is revealed by Him who is our Lord, it may yet be implicitly believed, and sacramentally minister of its own love, and joy, and peace, to those, who, though yet babes in Christ, have been baptized into it. It is confessedly a " mystery," that is a truth which cannot be explained by words alone, but must be grown up into by the communication of the same life, and through the experience of a certain discipline. [2]

And yet, though it is a mystery which is only " revealed from faith to faith," [3] saints have pointed out how much there is, even in present nature and in man, to reflect, though in imperfect and divided figures, something of the eternal undivided truth, which the " name of the Father, and of the Son, and of the Holy Ghost," declares to us. Temporal things,

---

[1] See the Greek or margin, 1 St. Pet. ii. 9.

[2] See Liddell and Scott's *Lexicon*, under the word μυστήριον.

[3] Rom. i. 17.

because they are broken and divided, cannot perfectly reveal what is eternal and undivided; and yet they may and do give us " shadows of the true," [1] which, though imperfect and divided, may help us to conceive how there can be a Son co-eval with the Father: how He can come forth, as the Word, to tell us of the Father and give us His Spirit, and yet ever abide in Him, in the unity of the same Spirit. Take the figure, which Scripture gives us, that " God is a sun," [2] and that " our God is a consuming fire." [3] In the sun we have first fire, then light, then heat; the light, differing from fire or heat, yet produced and brought forth by the fire; and the heat, differing from fire or light, yet proceeding from the fire. Yet these three are substantially one, as we can prove, and all are co-eval. But which of the three produces the others? Does the light or brightness come from the fire, or the fire from the brightness? The light or brightness comes from the fire, not the fire from the brightness. The fire produces the light. " Thus," as St. Augustine says, " the fire is the father of the light, and they are co-eval. Give me a fire without brightness, and I may believe that the Father ever was without the Son. . . . Shew me an eternal fire, and I will shew you an eternal light." [4] So, to take another illustration, which arises directly

---

[1] Heb. viii. 5; ix. 24; x. 1.

[2] Psalm lxxxiv. 11.   [3] Heb. xii. 29.

[4] Augustine, *Serm.* lxvii. § 11; (Ben. 117.) and *Serm.* lxviii. § 2; (Ben. 118.)

from our Lord's title as the "Word," who "in the beginning was with God, and was God."[1] Does not even man's word convey some hint, how a word may be in us, and yet come forth to convey to others what has been hidden in our hearts? I quote again from St. Augustine :—" Lo, the word which I am speaking to you I have had in my heart. It comes forth from me to you, and, if you receive it, it may enlighten and abide with you ; yet it does not leave me because it comes to you. Even so the Word may come forth to us from the Father, and yet not depart from Him. . . . And you may each and all receive the Word without division. If it were a cake of bread which I was giving to you, to take it in you would have to divide it, and each could only have a part. But in receiving a word, whether mine or God's, it comes whole to all and each. You may each have the whole, for the Word of God is whole everywhere."[2] I have already alluded to the constant argument of the same great Church teacher, that, if God is Love, there must be in Him a Lover, a Beloved, and the Spirit of Love ; for there is no love without a lover and a beloved :—" Ubi amor, ibi trinitas."[3] But even more striking are the considerations, which, as Augustine shews so fully, are suggested by the trinity in man, namely, of a will, a reason, and an affection,

---

[1] St. John i. 1.

[2] Augustine, *Serm.* lxix. § 7 ; (Ben. 119.) and *Serm.* lxx. § 3. (Ben. 120).

[3] See the viiith, ixth, and xth books of Augustine's *De Trinitate,* almost *passim.*

which, though three, are no less truly one.[1] I write however for those, who, because Christ says it, believe that " the Lord our God is One Lord, " though He is no less certainly " Father, Son, and Holy Ghost." If only we walk with Him, till heaven opens to us, and our hearts are truly knit together in love, we shall surely come into all the riches of the full as- surance of understanding, to the acknowledgment of the mystery of God, even of the Father, and of Christ, and His Spirit.

I will not conclude these notes on this last name of God, as revealed by the risen Christ to disciples upon whom He had breathed, and to whom He had said, " Receive ye the Holy Ghost," without noticing how this same name, in a slightly different form, is taught by the Apostle Paul to " babes in Christ," of whom he says, " I could not speak to you as unto spiritual, but as unto carnal," [2] who, unlike their teacher, as yet only " knew Christ after the flesh " [3] and were still full of their own " envyings and strifes," and " debates and backbitings." [4] To these " carnal " disciples the Apostle thus declares the Threefold Name :—" The grace of our Lord Jesus Christ, and the love of God, and the fellowship of the Holy Ghost, be with you all. Amen." [5] Need I point out how the order of the Persons in the

---

[1] See the ixth and xth, xiiith, and xivth books of the *De Trinitate*.

[2] 1 Cor. iii. 1.

[3] 2 Cor. v. 16.

[4] 1 Cor. iii. 3 ; 2 Cor. xii. 20.

[5] 2 Cor. xiii. 14.

Godhead here differs from the order as revealed by
the risen Lord to those who knew something of the
power of His resurrection.   This is not without a
purpose.   As in the Law of the Offerings of old, the
Sin and Trespass offerings, that is the view of Christ
as Sin-bearer, though last in order of institution,
were in order of use and application invariably prior
to the Sweet-savour offerings, which shewed Christ
in His sinless obedience, voluntarily yielding up
Himself to God in everything; [1] so in the revelation
of God's name, the knowledge of what He is for
sinners, and the course in which His grace and love
are now made known, is needed by carnal and imperfect souls before they can really receive the higher
truth of what He is in Himself in His eternal
generation.   Therefore to carnal souls the Apostle
says, "The grace of our Lord Jesus Christ, and the
love of God, and the fellowship of the Holy Ghost,
be with you.   Amen."   We are so familiar with the
words that we are in danger of overlooking all that
is taught in them, and what they imply as to the
state of those to whom they were addressed by the
Apostle.

For the words describe a growing experience.
As sinful creatures our first knowledge of God is
through "the grace of our Lord Jesus Christ."

---

[1] Compare Lev. i.–vii., which gives the order of institution,
with Exod. xxix.; Lev. viii., ix., and xiv.; and 2 Chron. xxix.;
which latter chapters give the order in which the sacrifices were
offered by God's people.

Awakened souls always begin here. We feel that
we are sinners; that we are lepers, palsied, fevered,
lame, or blind. We want some help and deliverance.
How are we to get it? We do not yet know God.
Till we have tasted of " the grace of our Lord Jesus
Christ," God is practically a stranger to us. So, in
one way or another, as poor, lost creatures, with more
or less knowledge of our need, we come or are brought
to Christ, or He comes to us, and we find " His grace
is sufficient for us." Observe, that it is " the grace
of our Lord Jesus Christ" with which the blessing
here commences. The Apostle does not say, " The
grace of the Son of God," though of course Jesus
Christ is Son of God. The deep mystery of the
Divine Sonship might be too deep for carnal souls.
Besides, when we first come or are brought to Christ,
our thoughts of Him are as of a " Lord," who has
power to save or judge us, rather than of His eternal
relation to the Father. At such a stage what we
chiefly need is to " know the grace of our Lord Jesus
Christ, that, though He was rich, yet for our sakes
He became poor." [1] As we see Him in the flesh, we
learn to see " the exceeding riches of His grace," [2]
and how it can save souls in every condition of will
or mind, and out of every form of plague and evil.
It cleanses the leper, who believed in His power, but
hardly in His will, to help; who said, " Lord, if thou
wilt, thou canst make me clean." [3] It casts the evil
spirit out of the man possessed with devils, whose

[1] 2 Cor. viii. 9.   [2] Eph. ii. 7.   [3] St. Matt. viii. 2.

father believed in Christ's will, but doubted His power; whose cry was, "If thou canst do anything, have compassion on us."[1]　It healed the paralytic, because of the faith of those who brought him.[2]　It raised the dead, without any faith, either on their own part, or in those about them.[3]　It delivered another demoniac, even against his shrinking from the Lord who healed him, and in spite of his prayers to be "let alone."[4]　It healed the ear of one who had come out only to seize and bind the Lord.[5]　It prayed even for those who slew the life which thus shewed grace to all.[6]　In all these and in countless other cases, "where sin abounded, grace did much more abound."[7]　And this "grace of our Lord Jesus Christ" is still the same. Blessed are they who know it.　Such know at least One Person of the ever-blessed Trinity.　And though as yet they may know Him most imperfectly, hardly knowing He is "Son of God," with the blind man of old they can now say, "One thing I know, that, whereas I was blind, now I see;"[8] for "of His fulness they have received, and grace for grace."[9]

But those who have got thus far will soon go further.　Jesus is "the way" to God.[10]　Souls, therefore, who know the "grace of our Lord Jesus Christ,"

---

[1] St. Mark ix. 22.　　　　　　　　[2] St. Matt. ix. 2.

[3] St. Luke vii. 13.

[4] St. Mark v. 7.　See also St. Mark i. 24 and St. Luke iv. 34.

[5] St. Luke xxii. 51.　　　　　　　[6] St. Luke xxiii. 34.

[7] Rom. v. 20.　　　　　　　　　　[8] St. John ix. 25, 35.

[9] St. John i. 16.　　　　　　　　　[10] St. John xiv. 6.

speedily come to know the " love of God." It is of course " the love of the Father," for Christ is witness that " God so loved the world that He gave His only-begotten Son, that whosoever believeth in Him should not perish, but have everlasting life." [1] But it is here seen as the " love of God." God thus " commendeth His love towards us, in that while we were yet sinners, Christ died for us." [2] " Hereby perceive we the love of God." [3] So we are brought to know another Person of the Blessed Trinity, and to " love Him, because He first loved us." There is much more that we have yet to learn ; but when by grace we have " peace with God," because " the love of God is shed abroad in our hearts " through Jesus Christ our Lord,[4] we can say with joy, " If God be for us, who can be against us ? He that spared not His own Son, but delivered Him up for us all, how shall He not with Him also freely give us all things ? " [5] Therefore the Apostle concludes touching this love,— " I am persuaded that neither death, nor life, nor angels, nor principalities, nor powers, nor things present, nor things to come, nor height, nor depth, nor any other creature, shall be able to separate us from the love of God, which is in Christ Jesus our Lord." [6]

There is yet more to know. Having thus learnt the " love of God," we may and shall come to the

---

[1] St. John iii. 16.
[2] Rom. v. 8.
[3] 1 St. John iii. 16.
[4] Rom. v. 1, 5.
[5] Rom. viii. 31, 32.
[6] Rom. viii. 38, 39.

" communion of the Holy Ghost " also; to know that
God's own Spirit has come to us, to " dwell in us,"
in dwellings which to Him must be full of foulness
and corruption ; not standing outside or afar off,
but even coming into sin-stained hearts, until He
" shall change our vile body, that it may be fashioned
like unto Christ's glorious body," [1] by such love prov-
ing that He is the Holy Ghost. For it is to a
" communion " that we are thus called, even the
" communion of the Holy Ghost; " to have One
always with us, who shares His riches with us, and
makes us partakers of His own Spirit,[2] while He no
less bears our burdens and helps our infirmities, by
making intercession for us.[3] What this " communion
of the Holy Ghost " did for saints of old is witnessed
by their works. Men walked in the consciousness,
not only that heaven would one day be their home,
but that even here this heaven was open to them.[4]
No need for them, like the heathen, by wizards and
consulters with familiar spirits,[5] to seek a communion
with the unseen, for which, so long as he is in self-
hood, man is unfit, and which, as sought in self-will,
can only hurt him. The " communion of the Holy
Ghost " gave man something far better, through the
" grace of the Lord Jesus" and the " love of God," even
" fellowship with the Father and with the Son," [6]
which practically silenced and swallowed up, as Aaron's

---

[1] Phil. iii. 21.   [2] 1 Cor. xii. 13.   [3] Rom. viii. 26.
[4] St. Luke iii. 21; St. John i. 51 ; Acts x. 11.
[5] Deut. xviii. 9–12; Isa. viii. 19.   [6] 1 St. John i. 3.

rod did the rods of the Egyptian magicians,[1] all
inferior methods of communion with the so-called
invisible. Such a " fellowship " was found to be something higher, and more powerful, and more true, than
all the wonders of the old-world magic ; for it witnessed that men were " heirs of God and joint heirs
with Christ ; " it brought them " to Mount Sion, the
city of the living God, to an innumerable company of
angels, and to the church of the first-born, which are
enrolled in heaven ; and to God, the judge of all, and
to the spirits of just men made perfect ; and to Jesus,
the mediator of the new covenant, and to the blood
of sprinkling, which speaketh better things than that
of Abel."[2] In such a " communion " men were taught,
as they could bear it, what God hath prepared for
them that love Him ; " things which eye hath not
seen, nor hath ear heard, but which are revealed by
God's Spirit." [3]   Blessed be God, the self-same Spirit
yet abides, to guide us into all truth, by taking of
the things of Christ and of God, and by shewing
them to us.[4]

Thus in different measures and in different ways is
the last great name of God, the name of " the Father,
the Son, and the Holy Ghost," revealed and opened to
believers ; some apprehending it as it unveils vital
relationships in God ; some, as it meets the need of
His creatures, who have fallen from Him.   In whatever measure it is received, it must give peace.   In

---

[1] Exod. vii. 12.

[2] Heb. xii. 22, 23.

[3] 1 Cor. iii. 9, 10.

[4] St. John xvi. 13, 15.

every age it has been true, that "they who know God's name will put their trust in Him." [1]   Much more should we, to whom by His beloved Son He has revealed Himself as "our Father," trust Him, and rest in Him, in every trial.   Shall we not pray, "Our Father, hallowed be thy name, thy kingdom come, thy will be done"? [2]   Shall we not bless Him for the assurance, that "all nations shall come and worship before Him, and shall glorify His name"? [3] Shall we not say, even while the conflict lasts, "Blessed be His glorious name for ever, and let the whole earth be filled with His glory.   Amen and Amen"? [4]

---

[1] Psalm ix. 10.

[2] St. Matt. vi. 9.

[3] Psalm lxxxvi. 9.

[4] Psalm lxxii. 19.

9

PARTAKERS OF THE DIVINE NATURE

WHAT is the Gospel? What are the "tidings of great joy" to be proclaimed to all as the substance or result of Christ's coming? Several answers might be given, differing somewhat in form, yet true. Some perhaps would say, This is the Gospel: —"Christ Jesus came into the world to save sinners:"[1] others, that "through this Man is preached unto you the forgiveness of sins; and by Him all that believe are justified from all things, from which they could not be justified by the law of Moses."[2] Others again would give the fuller statement in our Lord's own words, namely, that "God so loved the world, that He gave His Only-begotten Son, that whosoever believeth in Him should not perish, but have everlasting life."[3] These words surely are the Gospel, and implicitly contain all the "good news" which God, who spake at sundry times and divers manners unto the fathers by the prophets, hath in these last days spoken unto us by Him who

---

[1] 1 Tim. i. 15.   [2] Acts xiii. 38, 39.

[3] St. John iii. 16.

is the Son.   But is this, as men generally understand
it at least, the Gospel according to the Four Evan-
gelists?   What is the substance of what we rightly
call the Four Gospels?   Is it not, that, by the coming
of the Eternal Word, a New Man has been brought
forth out of our divided nature, who is truly Son of
God and Son of Man, the witness that the breach
which sin has made is healed, and that God has
come to dwell in man, so that man may do the works
of God, and that man has come to dwell in God?
Is not this the fact revealed in Christ?   But did the
" Only-begotten of the Father " become Man that He
should dwell alone as Son of God?   Was it not
rather that He should be the " Firstborn among
many brethren," who through Him should be sons
of God, and do His works, and manifest and minister
the same spirit? [1]   This is the good news which
makes the angels glad, even if men as yet only dimly
apprehend it.   We are called with this calling,
" that Christ should be formed in us," [2] that thus we
should be " partakers of the Divine nature." [3]   In
and by Him even now are we the sons of God.   It is
not yet made manifest what we shall be: but we

---

[1] The Early Church saw clearly the distinction between the
two apparently contradictory titles, " Only-begotten," and " First-
born."   The " Only-begotten " is the Son, prior to all division :
the " Firstborn " is " the male that first openeth the womb,"
(Exod. xiii. 12,) that is, the first delivered out of the fall or
separation.   So Athanasius, *Discourses against the Arians*, ii.
c. 21, § 9; also Theodoret, on Col. i. 15; and others.

[2] Gal. iv. 19 ; Col. i. 27.   [3] 2 St. Peter i. 4.

know that when He shall appear, we shall be like Him ; and even here, " as He is, so are we in this world." [1]

As a conclusion, therefore, to our meditations on the Names of God, which revealed to men of old, as they could bear it, His varied fulness, let us turn to see how all this fulness has been declared and seen in Christ, and may and shall be manifested in His living members, as they grow up in Him to bear His image.

First as to Christ.   Every virtue and relationship in God, revealed piecemeal in the Names which Holy Scripture gives us, comes into perfect manifestation in the life and death of the Only-begotten of the Father, of whose fulness we have received, and grace for grace.[2]   Let us take the Names in order.   Even a glance at them will shew that " Christ is all, and in all."

" Elohim " comes first, One whose name and ways declare a covenant-relation ; One therefore whose love can never change, because He loves in virtue of relationship.   Is not this name declared in Christ ? Does He only love us if we are lovely ; or does He not rather, as " Elohim," spite of all failings on our part, love us with unforsaking love, in virtue of a relationship which is not changed by our condition ? What does not Christ's life witness ?   The world was lost and helpless.   Men were all gone out of the way. Jews and Gentiles all were under sin.   But all were His, for " all things were created by Him and for

---

[1] 1 St. John iv. 17.   [2] St. John i. 16.

Him," [1] and as a "faithful Creator" [2] He can never leave them nor forsake them. "All that the Father hath," He says, "are mine." [3] Some indeed are His by a special bond, even those whom the Father has given Him as "first fruits," out of the world, [4] to be "members of His body, of His flesh, and of His bones." [5] These are His "chosen," [6] whom He calls "His sheep, who hear His voice, and follow Him." [7] And having loved these, He loves them to the end. But "other sheep He has, which are not of this fold. Them also He must bring, and they shall hear His voice, and there shall be one flock and one Shepherd." [8] For they are His, not by creation only, but bought with His precious blood; [9] and "the blood of the everlasting covenant" [10] is the witness that man is loved with an unchanging love, though for a season lost and fallen. Therefore Christ came; and ever since His coming He has been shewing how He loves, bringing light out of darkness, and order out of confusion; nor will He cease working until, as at the creation, God's image again is seen in man, and "all things are made new." [11]

Thus does Christ reveal "Elohim." But He no less manifests "Jehovah," who loves in virtue of

---

[1] Col. i. 16.
[2] 1 St. Peter iv. 19.
[3] St. John xvi. 15; and xvii. 10.
[4] St. James i. 18; Rev. xiv. 4.
[5] Eph. v. 30.
[6] Rev. xvii. 14.
[7] St. John x. 27, 28.
[8] St. John x. 16.
[9] 1 Tim. ii. 6; 1 Pet. i. 19.
[10] Heb. xiii. 20.
[11] Rev. xxi. 5.

quality, and " will by no means clear the guilty." [1]
The prophet who foresees that " He shall deliver the
needy, when he crieth ; the poor also, and him that
hath no helper ; " [2] no less declares that He " loveth
righteousness and hateth iniquity," [3] and that " He
cometh to judge the world with equity and the people
with His truth." [4] Some of His elect may think,
that, because they are elect, He will not judge them.
But because He is the Truth, He must judge all
wrong, and judge it even more in those who know
and are near Him, than in those who know Him not.
For He reveals Him who said of old, " You only have
I known of all the families of the earth : therefore
will I punish you for your iniquities." [5] He is indeed
perfect love to those, who by confession shew, that,
though ruined, they are true ; but He is no less unswerving truth and justice to such as would appear
what they are not, and cover sin by a cloak of reli-
giousness. Need I give examples from His words to
Pharisees and Scribes,[6] and still more to the Churches,
to whom He says, " I will give to every one of you
according to your works"? [7] To all He is the faithful
and true witness, whose eyes are as a flame of fire,
and out of whose mouth goeth the sharp two-edged
sword, to smite the nations.[8] And yet, with all this,

---

[1] Exod. xxxiv. 7. [2] Psalm lxxii. 12.
[3] Psalm xlv. 5, 7 ; Heb. i. 9.
[4] Psalm xcvi. 13. [5] Amos iii. 2.
[6] St. Matt. xxiii. 13–33. [7] Rev. ii. 23.
[8] Rev. ii. 11, 12, 18 ; iii. 14 ; and xix. 15.

His people's sin and judgment pain Him. Like "Jehovah," He suffers with, and grieves for, them. Again and again "He sighed,"[1] and "groaned in spirit,"[2] and "wept over Jerusalem, saying, If thou hadst known, in this thy day, the things which belong to thy peace;"[3] and again, "How often would I have gathered you, but ye would not."[4] Still more did He suffer, when "He himself bare our sins in His own body on the tree,"[5] thus making atonement for sinners by giving Himself to be their righteousness. In all such acts, He was revealing "Jehovah," who, if there is evil, must judge and take it away, even if He Himself is pained and suffers through the judgment.

Nor does our Lord less reveal "El Shaddai," the Almighty "Pourer-forth," who by the communication of His Spirit makes His servants fruitful through self-judgment. This was the name which Abram learnt "when he was ninety years old and nine,"[6] when, having failed to obtain the seed of promise in his own strength or by his fleshly energy, "El Shaddai" appeared, and by the communication of His own out-breath changed him from Abram into Abraham, and then, through circumcision—that is the judgment of his flesh—gave him the promised seed, with the assurance of still greater fruitfulness. But Christ fulfils this also. Surely He does this when

---

[1] St. Mark vii. 34; and viii. 12.   [2] St. John xi. 33, 38.
[3] St. Luke xix. 41, 42.   [4] St. Matt. xxiii. 37.
[5] 1 St. Peter ii. 24.   [6] Gen. xvii. 1.

He says, " He that eateth me shall live by me ; " when
He gives us "His flesh and blood, that He may
abide in us and we in Him ; " [1] that so abiding, as
branches in the vine, we may, " being purged by Him,
bring forth much fruit." [2]   Still more He gives us of
His own powers, when having known Him for a
season only in the flesh, like the disciples of old before
the day of Pentecost, we are brought through the
"little while" of " sorrow," [3] to know Him in the
Spirit, [4] when He " pours out His Spirit," [5] for which
He bids us "tarry," [6] and when by it we "receive
power to be witnesses for Him," [7] and to do His works
and minister His Spirit.   Then, even as " He by the
eternal Spirit offered Himself to God," [8] pouring out
His very life-blood that we should live through Him,
they who drink into the same Spirit are willing, even
as He, to be poured out even to death to bless and
strengthen others. [9]   All this Christ gives us as partakers of His flesh and of His blood.   But both these
precious gifts involve self-judgment or God's judgment.   They who receive them unworthily "eat and
drink their own damnation." [10]   Therefore He calls
us to "judge ourselves that we be not judged of the
Lord."   But what is all this but the revelation of
" El Shaddai," who says, " Walk before me, and be

---

[1] St. John vi. 56, 57.   [2] St. John xv. 2, 5, 16.
[3] St. John xvi. 19-23.
[4] 2 Cor. v. 16 ; and Rom. i. 3-5.   [5] Acts ii. 17, 33.
[6] St. Luke xxiv. 49.   [7] Acts i. 8.
[8] Heb. ix. 14.   [9] Acts xxi. 13; 2 Tim. iv. 6.
[10] 1 Cor. xi. 29 ; Heb. x. 29.

thou perfect, and I will multiply thee exceedingly, and my covenant shall be in your flesh for an everlasting covenant."[1]

And does not our Lord equally reveal "El Elyon" or the "Most High," who has a "priesthood after the order of Melchisedek," and is thus linked, not with the elect only, but with all men? Was not this the message of the Angel at His birth?—"Behold, I bring you good tidings of great joy, which shall be to all people."[2] Was not this the vision which made old Simeon glad, when he said, "Lord, now lettest thou thy servant depart in peace; for mine eyes have seen thy salvation, which thou hast prepared before the face of all people; a light to lighten the Gentiles, and to be the glory of thy people Israel"?[3] Christ, as the revealer of God, fills many relationships, but none grander than that He is Man, and as Man is related, not to the elect only, but to all men. For indeed God is related to all men, for "Adam was son of God." Therefore the Gospel, which specially reveals our Lord as Son of Man, with distinct purpose traces His descent from God through Adam.[4] Man is son of God, though he knows it not, and in and through Christ inherits a priesthood, which, like that of Melchisedek, rests not on law, but on relationship. Still more does our Lord reveal the "Most High," "Possessor of heaven and earth," in that, having humbled Himself, God

---

[1] Gen. xvii. 1, 2, 11, 13.
[2] St. Luke ii. 10.
[3] St. Luke ii. 29, 31.
[4] St. Luke iii. 22, 38.

hath greatly exalted Him, and made Him "Prince
of the kings of the earth," [1] King as well as Priest,
"Head of all principality and power," [2] and "Head
of every man." [3] "All things are put under Him,"
and yet "He is not ashamed to call us brethren; for
both He that sanctifieth and they that are sanctified
are all of one." [4] What is all this but the revelation
of the "Most High," who has acknowledged man
as partaker of His nature, saying, "Israel is my
son, my firstborn;" [5] and again, "Ye are gods, and
all of you children of the Most High"?

Thus does our Lord reveal "Elohim," "Jehovah,"
the "Almighty," and the "Most High." Need I
shew how He no less reveals "Adonai," "Master and
Husband," and the "God of Ages," and the "LORD
of Hosts"? Is not our universal use of the title
"Lord," as applied to Christ, the witness how deeply
the truth of His Lordship has penetrated men's
hearts? To us He is indeed "Adonai," our "Lord."
We "call Him Master, for so He is." [6] His we are,
and Him we serve. [7] He commits to each their
varied talents, for which they must give an account,
for every gift brings its special responsibility. But
He is more than "Master." He is "Husband." The
marriage of the Lamb is coming, when His Bride
will make herself ready; [8] and even now, as the

---

[1] Rev. i. 5.

[3] 1 Cor. xi. 3.

[5] Exod. iv. 22.

[7] Acts xxvii. 23.

[2] Col. ii. 10.

[4] Heb. ii. 8–11.

[6] St. John xiii. 13.

[8] Rev. xix. 7.

Apostle says, we are " espoused to Christ as to a husband." [1] Thus does He reveal " Adonai." But He is no less " El Olam," " Age-working God." Christ is witness how God works, and that by stages and degrees He speaks the word and gives His Spirit as men can bear it. He has many things to say, which disciples, while they are carnal, cannot bear. [2] Therefore He comes in the flesh and in fleshly forms, and speaks by parables and signs, till men can know Him in the Spirit. Thus too He accepts circumcision, and the temple-service, and the baptism of John, as stages to opened heavens, and transfiguration, and resurrection; shewing that " there is a season and a time for every purpose under heaven," [3] and that God in Christ is still " El Olam," while He is no less " LORD of Hosts," even of angels, who serve Him first and last; for, as the Apostle says, " When the Father bringeth the First-begotten into the world, He saith, And let all the angels of God worship Him." [4]

All this is generally seen. As Christians we all confess, that " the Son " is " the image of the invisible God," and that " the Only-begotten of the Father hath revealed Him." What is less clearly seen is, that Christ's members must likewise reveal Him, like their Lord and Head, in all His virtues and relationships. Let us note what the Scripture shews us of the saints, that we may better under-

[1] 2 Cor. xi. 3.
[2] St. John xvi. 12.
[3] Eccl. iii. 1.
[4] Heb. i. 5, 6.

stand what it is to be "imitators of God as dear children."[1]

And, first, must not Christ's members, like their Head, reveal "Elohim"? Are we not to love and work for all, however ruined they may be, not in virtue of their deserts, but because as God's creatures they are related to us? "Doth not nature teach us"[2] to love our own, though deformed, or lame, or blind, and even to love them more because of their infirmities? Much more are God's elect set in the world to love as they have been loved, and to forgive even as they have been forgiven. Therefore we see the Apostle, blessing though reviled, intreating though defamed, to the very end labouring for the lost, and saying, "I will very gladly spend and be spent for you, though the more abundantly I love you, the less I be loved."[3] As Christ had toiled for him, he toiled for others, in the faith that by a loving will and a true word all things can and shall be "made new."[4] But all this is the revelation of "Elohim," who worked unforsakingly on a ruined world, till in the place of darkness and confusion all was very good.

Nor do the saints less reveal "Jehovah," who loves righteousness. Look at the Apostles Peter and Paul. "Great grace was upon the Church, neither was there any among them that lacked, for as many as were possessors of lands and houses sold them, and

---

[1] Eph. v. i.

[2] 1 Cor. xi. 14.

[3] 1 Cor. iv. 12, 13; and 2 Cor. xii. 15.

[4] Rev. xxi. 5.

distribution was made to every man according as he had need." But two, professing to give all, "kept back a part," and thus "lied to the Holy Ghost." At once Peter judges the falsehood, saying, "How is it that ye have agreed together to tempt the Spirit of the Lord : thou hast not lied unto men, but unto God." And Ananias and his wife, hearing these words, fell down and died.[1] So again with Paul, when he was come to Paphos, and a certain false prophet withstood him, seeking to turn away the Deputy from the faith, the Apostle, filled with the Holy Ghost, said, " O full of all subtilty and malice, thou child of the devil, thou enemy to all righteousness, wilt thou not cease to pervert the right ways of the Lord ? And now, behold, the hand of the Lord is upon thee, and thou shalt be blind, not seeing the sun for a season." And immediately the wrongdoer was smitten with blindness.[2] So again at Corinth, while, as we have seen, there is the most unwearying love in the Apostle, so that he is willing to be "as the filth of the earth, and the offscouring of all things," if only thus he may serve his weak brethren,[3] there is no less the unswerving righteousness of the LORD, in the delivery of the fornicator to Satan, " for the destruction of his flesh, that his spirit may be saved in the day of the Lord Jesus." [4] It is so all through his course. He is loving, but he is righteous also. Witness such words as, " Shall I come to you with a rod" ? [5]

---

[1] Acts iv. 33–35; v. 1–11.   [2] Acts xiii. 6–11.
[3] 1 Cor. iv. 9–13.   [4] 1 Cor. v. 1-5.   [5] 1 Cor. iv. 21.

" Put away from yourselves that wicked person." [1]
" What fellowship hath righteousness with unrighteousness, and what communion hath light with darkness ? Wherefore come out and be separate, saith
the Lord, and touch not the unclean thing." [2] In
all this, and in other like words of the Apostle, we
see " Jehovah," who " will by no means clear the
guilty."

And yet, like the same " Jehovah," Paul's heart
is grieved by the sin of those whom he thus rebukes.
So he says, " Out of much affliction and anguish of
heart I wrote unto you with many tears ; not that
ye should be grieved, but that ye might know the
love which I have more abundantly unto you. For
if I make you sorry, who is he that maketh me glad,
but the same which is made sorry by me ? " [3] So
again, in his parting address to the Elders of Ephe-
sus, he refers to his " many tears," and to his service
among them " night and day with tears." [4] For the
faithful servant, like his Lord, while he must judge
all disobedience, suffers even with the judged. Who
is weak, and he is not weak ? Who is offended, and
he burns not ? [5]

Nor is " El Shaddai," the " Pourer-forth," less
seen in God's true saints, who, " being enriched in
everything to all bountifulness," [6] pour out to others
that which they have first received from the Almighty

---

[1] 1 Cor. v. 13.

[2] 2 Cor. vi. 14–17.

[3] 2 Cor. ii. 2–4.

[4] Acts xx. 19, 31.

[5] 2 Cor. x. 6 ; and xi. 29.

[6] 2 Cor. ix. 11.

Giver. This view of God's elect meets us at every turn throughout the New Testament. "I have fed you," says St. Paul, "with milk and not with meat, for hitherto ye were not able to bear it."[1] "We were gentle among you, even as a nurse cherisheth her children: so, being affectionately desirous of you, we were willing to have imparted unto you, not the Gospel of God only, but also our own souls, because ye were dear to us."[2] As themselves filled with the Spirit, the Apostles ministered it to those, who through self-judgment were prepared to receive what the " Almighty " still gives to those who " walk before Him." Thus, sometimes by the laying on of hands,[3] sometimes by preaching,[4] sometimes by prayer,[5] they were the channels by which God's fulness was poured out, on such as by the experience of their own helplessness had been prepared for it. The " manifestation of the Spirit " was given to them, and they " ministered the Spirit,"[6] that the Church might be built up, not by the works of the flesh, but by the fruits of God's Spirit. It is so yet. Now and to the end the true elect must be " pourers-forth," and " minister the Spirit," though now as of old it is the empty only who are filled, while the rich are sent empty away.

The next name, " Most High," as we might expect from its special connexion with the non-elect,

---

[1] 1 Cor. iii. 2.

[2] 1 Thess. ii. 7, 8.

[3] Acts viii. 17.

[4] Acts x. 44.

[5] Acts i. 14 ; and ii. 2–4.

[6] Gal. iii 5.

has as yet been less apprehended by the Church and by believers generally than those other names of God, which, as they were earlier revealed in Scripture, are even now more easily learnt and received by God's people.   But in every age, there have been saints, who, though of the election, have known this name, and, like Abram, have witnessed to the world that the "Most High" is indeed "Possessor of heaven and earth."   This was very specially the calling of the Apostle Paul, "to whom was committed the Gospel of the uncircumcision,"[1] and who, though rejected for it, testified to his brethren,[2] that God had a purpose far wider than the election, and that "in Abraham's seed, all nations should be blessed." For he had learnt, that there was a "priesthood after the order of Melchisedek," differing from and greater than that of the elect.   Therefore he said, "I am a debtor both to the Greeks and to the Barbarians; both to the wise and to the unwise;"[3] for "there is no difference between the Jew and the Greek; for the same Lord over all is rich unto all that call upon Him; for whosoever shall call upon the name of the Lord shall be saved."[4]   Therefore with heathen Athenians he could adopt the words of their own poet, and tell them that they were "God's offspring," for "God had made of one blood all nations of men that dwell on the face of the earth, that they should seek the Lord, and find Him, who is not far from

---

[1] Gal. ii. 7, 8.   [2] Acts xxii. 21, 22.
[3] Rom. i. 14.   [4] Rom. x. 12, 13.

any one of us." [1]   Even the Apostle of the circumcision had learnt this truth :—" God hath shewed me," he said to Cornelius, " that I should call no man common or unclean." [2]   And from that day to this there have been believers, who have learnt the same, and who, though judged as Paul was for his Gospel, can yet, like him, " give thanks for all men," [3] in the faith that the " Most High " is the " Possessor both of heaven and earth," and that, " of Him, and through Him, and to Him, are all things." [4]

I need but glance at the three remaining names of God, to shew how the elect, as they grow up in Christ, reveal them all, and shall yet more reveal them in the coming kingdom. They reveal " Adonai," " Lord ; " for though " the elders in the Church, who feed the flock," may not behave themselves " as lords over God's heritage," [5] yet are they called to " rule," [6] and if they " rule well," are " worthy of double honour," [7] and brethren are commanded to " obey and to be subject to them." [8]   Thus they manifest " Adonai," in ruling and directing others.   Much more shall they reveal Him when one shall be set " over ten cities," another " over five," [9] because they have " watched for souls, as those that must give an account," and have faithfully cared for and guided those committed to them.   And no less do God's

---

[1] Acts xvii. 26–28.

[2] Acts x. 28.

[3] 1 Tim. ii. 1.

[4] Rom. xi. 36.

[5] 1 St. Peter v. 1–3.   [6] Rom. xii. 8.   [7] 1 Tim. v. 17.

[8] Heb. xiii. 17.

[9] St. Luke xix. 17, 19.

true saints reveal " El Olam," the " Everlasting " or
" Age-working God," who has dealt with fallen men
as they could bear it, first without law, then under
law, and then under grace, like a Father meeting His
children where they are, and bearing with their
infirmities, till they are prepared for better things.
Pharisees or Separatists indeed, who " thank God
that they are not as other men," [1] may cut away all
the rounds of the ladder which are below them, con-
tending that the stage which they have reached is
the only one which God accepts, thus wronging those,
who, being yet babes, still need the lower forms of
truth, which alone can be received while men are
carnal. Not so those who are like Christ, who came,
and yet comes, in the flesh. Such can " become as
Jews to gain the Jews," and as " weak to gain the
weak," [2] " feeding them with milk and not with
meat," [3] knowing that there is a time even with
Christ for " Jewish water-pots," " set after the manner
of the purifying of the Jews ; " for the " water " can
be " turned to wine," when " the hour is come " for
the present Lord to " manifest forth His glory." [4]
And so with the title " LORD of Hosts." Some of
Christ's members may not yet know, that in and with
Him they share His place, as " far above all principality and power," [5] and that even here holy angels
wait on them,[6] while in the coming kingdom they

---

[1] St. Luke xviii. 11.

[2] 1 Cor. ix. 20, 22.

[3] 1 Cor. iii. 1, 2.

[4] St. John ii. 5–11.

[5] Eph. i. 20, 21.

[6] Heb. i. 14.

shall "judge angels." [1] Yet this is the calling of
God's sons. The hosts of heaven serve them. It is
only " for a little while " that " man is made lower
than the angels." [2]

Thus are the elect, even as their Lord, set here
to manifest the virtues, which they possess as " partakers of the divine nature," and which they shall
yet more manifest in the coming kingdom, when,
delivered from "the bondage of corruption," they
shall be " clothed upon " with their incorruptible and
perfect " house from heaven." As yet indeed many
are babes ; some are still unborn, though quickened
with God's life : what is seen of them is still nature
only, not the Lord. Such can manifest little or
nothing of their Father. But there are others, who
in their measure, though they do not yet apprehend
that for which they are apprehended, are shewing
forth something at least of the varied grace and
truth, which is theirs as sons and heirs of God.
How are they welcomed by the Church and world ?
Christ and His saints are the answer. They are
welcomed as God is welcomed. Who want or care
for God, till in some need or trial they find that they
are not and cannot be self-sufficient ? For God is
not known. Some dreadful misrepresentation of
Him keeps souls from Him, or men's pride and self-
love makes them averse to that which even nature
tells them of Him. So with His saints : " the world
knoweth them not, even as it knew Him not." [3]

---

[1] 1 Cor. vi. 3.　　　　[2] Heb. ii. 7.　　　　[3] 1 St. John iii. 1.

They may live and die for others; but their light
and love, because even without a word it is ever
judging all untruth and self-love, make them an
offence; and therefore they are rejected. Let those
who live out God's life understand their calling. So
long indeed as the life of God, though quickened, is
unseen in man, it offends none, for, like an unborn
child, it is yet unmanifested. Even when it is first
brought forth, and is still a babe, though it may
cause trouble to some,[1] yet, like Christ, it grows here
for a season, not in wisdom and stature only, but
" in favour also with God and man." [2]   As yet there
is nothing in such a life to judge others. Not so
after heaven opens; for then, because the Spirit of
the Father rests upon His sons, and His grace and
truth, not only are in, but also daily beaming forth
from, them, because this light exposes all pretences,
and this love condemns all self-love, those in whom
it is seen will be counted, as their Master, " breakers
of the law," [3] or " mad," [4] or " deceivers," [5] by those,
who, with much zeal for God, are yet in self-hood.

For truth is welcome only to the true : love is
welcome only to the loving.   Thus the " poor of the
flock," [6] who feel their need, are ever readier to
welcome and receive God's life, when it appears
among them, than the Pharisees and Scribes, who

---

[1] St. Matt.   3.   [2] St. Luke ii. 52.
[3] St. John v. 10.   [4] St. John x. 20.
[5] St. Matt. xxvii. 63 ; St. John vii. 12.
[6] Zech. xi. 11.

are satisfied with their own supposed attainments.
And yet this life, though despised of men, as unknown, yet well known, as sorrowful, yet always
rejoicing, as poor, yet making many rich, because it
is God's own life in flesh and blood, as in Christ the
Head, so in His members, must conquer all; not by
force, but by the cross, that is by patient suffering,
even unto death ; " by pureness, by knowledge, by
longsuffering, by kindness, by the Holy Ghost, by
love unfeigned, by the word of truth, by the power
of God," [1] commending God to those who yet are far
from Him.   Therefore let God's sons rejoice, that as
Christ is, so are they in this world.   It is but a little
while and the glory of the Lord shall be revealed,
and all flesh shall see it together.   " Then shall the
righteous shine forth as the sun in the kingdom of
their Father.   Who hath ears to hear let him hear."

[1] 2 Cor. vi. 6–10.

APPENDIX

In the preceding Lectures I have referred in passing to the objections which have been urged against the unity and Divine inspiration of Holy Scripture, based chiefly, or to a great extent, on the varied names of God, more particularly the names, " Elohim," and " Jehovah," which alternate so remarkably throughout the Pentateuch. My object was not to enter on the question of the nature and inspiration of the Bible ; for I was addressing believers, who accepted Christ's words as truth, that " no jot or tittle of the law should fail," and that, though " heaven and earth should pass away, His words should not pass away." I rather desired to open to my brethren what the Lord by grace had opened to me, of the riches of that Word or Book, which the Apostle describes as " a light that shineth in a dark place,"[1] and which I had long proved to be " a lamp unto my feet, and a light unto my path." [2] Of course I was aware of the so-called " conclusions " of " scientific criticism." I had weighed them again and again, only to be increasingly astonished at the recklessness of assertion and

---

[1] 2 St. Peter i. 19.　　　　[2] Psalm cxix. 105.

assumption, which takes the place of proof with some on this question. But believing that error is ever better answered simply by the truth than by pursuing and running down the falsehood, I did not care, in these pages at least, to enter into any detail of what I am convinced is a mistake, though, like most mistakes, it may contain a measure of perverted truth in it.

I may however add here a few lines to note what appears to me the fundamental error of the critics and their so-called " scientific criticism." Not one of them, so far as my experience goes, seems ever to have considered under what conditions a Divine revelation can be given to fallen creatures, or the qualifications necessary to recognise and rightly apprehend such a revelation. Hence these critics have acted, and could not but act, just like the Jews of old, who stumbled at the human form of the Divine Word, and therefore unhesitatingly judged and rejected it, though, to those who felt their need, that Incarnate Word had abundantly ministered health and deliverance, through the very form which learned scribes only mocked and stripped and crucified. For in mercy to lost men, and to reach them where they were, the Word of God had come in a form, whose earthly lineage could be plainly proved, and whose susceptibility to injury was manifest to all. Therefore its judges assumed, and thought they had proved, that it could not be Divine. Just so, and for the same reasons, has the Written Word been judged. But " the Scripture cannot be broken."

As surely as Christ rose, and ministered to men His Spirit, so will His Word in Holy Scripture conquer all, spite of all the judgments of those who brand it as a " Deceiver."

The fact is that every one of the objections which so-called " scientific criticism " has brought against the Bible,—that it is an outcome of man's heart, and has grown with men, and bears their likeness, and is therefore marked throughout with man's infirmities,— may equally be brought, not only against the Incarnation, but in substance also against the books of Nature and Providence; so that the Incarnation, and Nature, and Providence, may all be arraigned at the bar of man's understanding, as bearing proofs that they are faulty, and cannot be of God. Look at the Incarnation. What would learned men have found in Christ's body, had they, instead of endeavouring to learn from it as a living Teacher, only dissected it as a dead thing, as the scientific critics have been so busy dissecting Scripture? Would they have found, with the eye of sense at least, that that body had been divinely formed, and was in a very special way God's chosen tabernacle? Could not the dissectors have shewn that it was human, born of an earthly mother, and bearing in its form marks, not only of her likeness, but of those from whom she came, that is, that it was of Jewish lineage; nay, might they not have gone further, and proved that the very particles it was composed of had, before they became parts of the body of the Lord, been component parts, either of some animal or vegetable, and concluded that therefore that Human Form could not possibly be Divine ? In like manner might it not be said, that, as Nature is manifestly composed of heterogeneous substances, thrown together into their present form, to the eye of sense at least, with no little confusion, and with marks that they have all pre-existed in some other form, such a fact is proof that even Nature cannot be the handiwork of God. Certainly whatever may be said against the Bible, on the score that it is, or may have been, made up of previously existing materials, may no less be urged against Nature and the Flesh of Christ, both of which have in them precisely the same peculiarities. It is just the same with Providence, which may be and has been arraigned by some as guilty of acts unworthy of a God, and which, if done by men, would bring them to the gallows. What then ? Is not Christ's flesh of God ? Is not Nature also His building ? Is not Providence His work, spite of its many apparent anomalies ? And does not the fact, that Holy Scripture has the same apparent anomalies, which are indeed marks of the state of the creature whom it is meant to serve, witness that the one even as the others, though there yet are mysteries in all, is the work of the same One Divine Artificer ? Let not believers be afraid. The books of God are not going to fail, because " scientific criticism " has been so learnedly busy, and declares itself dissatisfied with them.

In truth the criticism of the critics is so open to correction, and is often based on such mere assertion and assumption, that almost every fresh critic finds something to correct and judge in all his predecessors. As with the rejectors of the Christ too, "their witness does not agree." But what will not unbelief believe, especially when it boasts its superior wisdom and enlightenment? It might astonish a simple Christian to know that the Book which has for ages fed the Church, and which has been teaching, and successfully teaching, righteousness and truth, as no other book has ever taught these, is, according to the critics, based throughout on fraud and falsehood, merely the work of a " Jehovist," and of an " Elohist," improved by a " second Elohist," then by a " Deuteronomist," and lastly by some unknown " Redactor," till it has become the confused and heterogeneous thing which it now is in the eyes of critics, fit only to be condemned and demolished by their criticism. Well may the Apostle ask, " Where is the wise? Where is the scribe? Where is the disputer of this world? Hath not God made foolish the wisdom of this world?"

For, spite of the critics, the Book, in its grandeur and fulness, still lives, and goes on feeding hungry souls, and giving living waters for the thirsty. There it stands, as saints have seen, human and yet no less Divine, meeting men at every stage, in forms which they can profit by; in the letter full of lessons for our guidance through this present world, while in

spirit it reveals yet veils the depths of God's wisdom.
I will not repeat here what I have said elsewhere as
to the way in which the Bible, in its varied books,
having first shewn us all the outcome of Adam, gives
us instruction as to every stage of the appointed way
out of the Fall, shewing our dangers, our failures,
our deliverances, and our sins, till out of every bondage, every wandering, every conflict, and every sin,
man is brought even through death into the new
creation and the heavenly city of his God.   Every
fact recorded, nay, every word, is to the opened eye
a revelation, not only from God, but of God, shewing,
in the oft-repeated and manifold discovery of the
creatures' need, the unfailing fulness of that grace
and truth, which is indeed sufficient for us and all
creatures.

I cannot go into all this here.   It will be sufficient
to remind believers that, in the Gospels, our Lord
again and again speaks of Moses as the author of the
books which have always gone by his name;   and
connects with him the legislation which our modern
critics refer to the so-called " Jehovist," the " Elohist,"
and the " Deuteronomist," and to widely different and
even post-exilian periods.   The following are some of
our Lord's allusions to the law; first to the law of
leprosy; St. Matt. viii. 4; St. Mark i. 44; St. Luke
v. 14: then as to divorce; St. Matt. xix. 8; and St.
Mark x. 3, 9: then as to reverence for parents; St.
Mark vii. 10: then as to resurrection; St. Luke xx.
37: then as to circumcision; St. John vii. 22, 23:

then as to the brazen serpent; St. John iii. 14 : and
to the bread from heaven; St. John vi. 32. In other
passages, as in St. Matt. xxiii. 2, and St. John vii. 19,
Moses and his law are referred to, without any distinct
commandment being specified. In three other places,
namely St. Mark xii. 26 ; St. Luke xvi. 29, 31 ; and
xxiv. 44, our Lord, speaking of the Old Testament,
either in whole or in part, refers to it as the " Book
of Moses," " Moses and the Prophets," or " the law
of Moses, the Prophets, and the Psalms ; " and lastly,
in St. John v. 45–47, He again appeals to the " writings of Moses," as witnessing of Him, telling the
Jews, that " if they believed Moses, they would also
believe Him, for Moses wrote of Him." All this is
nothing to the critics. We cannot therefore be sur-
prised that the witness of the Apostles, who in not
less than some thirty places refer the Pentateuch to
Moses, or quote it as of Divine authority, should be
set aside as curtly as the testimony of our Lord.
And all this in the country of Luther! Faith in the
Church has long since been gone : faith in the Scriptures is fast going. How long will even the pro-
fession of faith in Christ remain ? Men must be
asleep or blind if they do not see what is fast coming
upon Christendom.

In conclusion may I say, that I believe one main
cause of objections to the Bible lies in its power over
man's conscience ? The Book will speak for God,
whether men will hear or whether they will forbear.
But all critics are not so open as the poor East-end lec-

turer, who, when asked by one of his hearers,—" Why is all your criticism turned against the Bible, instead of against Shakspeare or Homer? Why don't you let the Bible alone?" replied with English outspokenness,—" Why don't I let the Bible alone? Because the Bible won't let me alone." It ever has been a witness for God, and still will be, while men need light in a dark place. When that which is perfect is come, then that which is in part shall be done away.

Meanwhile be it remembered, that, as the Bible was written by men, to whom the spirit-world had been more or less opened, and who spake as they were moved by the Holy Ghost, it can never be fully understood, except by those to whom the same world is now opened by the same Spirit. The great opening is even now at hand. Blessed are they who by grace are waiting for it.

BY THE SAME AUTHOR

THE LAW OF THE OFFERINGS   **Andrew Jukes**

The standard work on the subject of the Tabernacle offerings and their typical significance. Andrew Jukes masterfully and clearly explains the offerings and their application to the New Testament believer. Exposition is given in depth of all five Levitical offerings as well as the entire sacrificial system.

"A classic on the typological significance of the offerings mentioned in Leviticus, showing how each clearly points toward some particular aspect of the redemptive work of Christ."
   —David W. Brookman, *Basic Books for the Minister's Library*

"No one explains the significance of the Levitical offerings (in relation to Calvary) as well as Jukes does here. . . . Suddenly . . . it bursts into life with several superb chapters which are practically essential to the study of Leviticus."
—Peter M. Masters, Pastor, Metropolitan Tabernacle (Spurgeon's)

"A very condensed, instructive, refreshing book. It will open up new trains of thought to those unversed in the teaching of the types."   —Charles H. Spurgeon, *Commenting and Commentaries*

ISBN 0-8254-2958-7   234 pp.   paperback